D1611024

Improving teaching and learning in the core curriculum

LOOKING AFRESH AT THE PRIMARY CURRICULUM SERIES

Series Editors: Kate Ashcroft and David James,
               University of West of England, Bristol

Improving teaching and learning in the humanities
Edited by Martin Ashley

Improving teaching and learning in the core curriculum
Edited by Kate Ashcroft and John Lee

Improving teaching and learning in the arts
Edited by Mary Kear and Gloria Callaway

Improving teaching and learning in the core curriculum

Edited by Kate Ashcroft and John Lee

FALMER PRESS
· Taylor & Francis Group ·

First published 2000 by Falmer Press
11 New Fetter Lane, London EC4P 4EE

Simultaneously published in the USA and Canada
by Falmer Press
Routledge Inc, 29 West 35th Street, New York, NY 10001

Falmer Press is an imprint of the Taylor & Francis Group

Typeset in Melior by Graphicraft Limited, Hong Kong
Printed and bound in Great Britain by TJ International Ltd, Padstow,
Cornwall

British Library Cataloguing in Publication Data
A catalogue record for this book is available from the British Library

Library of Congress Cataloging in Publication Data
Improving teaching and learning in the core curriculum / edited by
   Kate Ashcroft and John Lee.
         p.   cm. — (Developing primary practice series)
      Includes bibliographical references and index.
      1. Education, Elementary—Great Britain—Curricula.
   2. Curriculum planning—Great Britain.   I. Ashcroft, Kate.
   II. Lee, John, 1944– .   III. Series.
   LB1564.G7I475   1999   99–28037
   372.19′0941—dc21

Cover design by Carla Turchini

ISBN 0–7507–0813–1

Contents

CONTENTS

List of figures and tables

Acknowledgments

We should like to thank: Liz Shearer and the children from Eastcombe Primary School; third year English students from the Faculty of Education, UWE 1998.

Glossary

Antonym	a word that is the opposite to another word (good–bad)
Deixis	from the Greek word for 'pointing'
	Features of language that refer to the personal, temporal or spatial characteristics of a situation; deitic forms include: 'you', 'now', 'this', 'there'
Genre	refers to ways in which texts have similarities and differences; typical instances are stories, scientific reports, and arguments
Grammar	one of three components of language structure, the other two being phonology and semantics
Metalanguage	the language used to talk about language
Standard English	the prestigious dialect of English that is usually used in print and is taught in schools and to non-native speakers learning English. It is used in broadcasts, in education, in professional life and formal situations
Synonym	a word that has the same meaning as another word (big–large)
Text	a complete stretch of language either spoken or written with a definable communicative function

Series editors' preface and introduction

Kate Ashcroft and David James

Improving teaching and learning in the core curriculum is one of a series of books in the Looking Afresh at the Primary Curriculum Series edited by Kate Ashcroft and David James. Other books in the series include;

- *Improving teaching and learning in the arts*, edited by Mary Kear and Gloria Callaway; and
- *Improving teaching and learning in the humanities*, edited by Martin Ashley.

Like the other books in the series, *Improving teaching and learning in the core curriculum* is written as an essential support for students training in colleges and universities for primary teaching, those undertaking in-service teacher education and teachers in schools wishing to use an accessible text to get in touch with some of the more recent thinking about the primary curriculum. It is a natural 'next step' from the two introductory texts published by Falmer Press, that cover the whole curriculum:

- *The Primary Teacher's Guide to the New National Curriculum*, edited by Kate Ashcroft and David Palacio; and
- *Implementing the Primary Curriculum*, edited by Kate Ashcroft and David Palacio.

The present book is intended to build on and further develop knowledge about the curriculum that was included at an introductory level in the two books above and, in particular, asks the reader to look in more depth at the link between the core curriculum subjects and children's learning in schools. It is aimed at supporting students and teachers who are beginning to get to grips with what it means to be a curriculum specialist for one of the National Curriculum subjects in a primary school.

The book could be used in various ways. It will be of use for teachers and student teachers wishing to gain an overview of aspects of teacher education programmes related to the core curriculum. It is also designed to be used by student teachers at the stage when they are beginning that part of their course that applies to the role of a core curriculum specialist in the primary school. The enquiry-based format provides a starting point for the sort of enquiry, reflection and learning that tutors are trying to encourage within initial teacher education and in-service courses based on the Reflective Teacher Model.

The book is well signposted with headings and sub-headings, with lots of practical suggestions of ways of going about curriculum planning, reflection and enquiry. There is some reference to theory, but wherever possible, this is illustrated with practical examples in the form of Case Studies that highlight implications for the enquiring teacher.

The book does not aim to present a series of outcomes of research to be absorbed by teachers, nor does it focus on their skills as educational researchers *per se*; nor does it attempt to give a list of tips. It is focused on enquiry with a view to improving practice through:
■ accessible content at the reader's level about the main issues;
■ knowledge about a range of teaching methods and curriculum content;
■ knowledge about the way information and communicative technologies can influence teaching, learning and curriculum content;
■ enquiry tasks that encourage the reader to:
– assess and develop their understandings of the issues,
– assess and develop their subject knowledge,
– try out activities in the classroom and collect data about their effects and effectiveness;
■ an annotated reading list at the end of each chapter.

Although some of the ideas contained in the book are complex and could be seen as demanding, the authors have been careful to keep the style of the books as straightforward as possible. They have kept sentences and paragraphs short and made the language accessible rather than 'academic'. Wherever possible, new ideas and concepts are supported by concrete examples. The authors' intention is to communicate clearly some of the complexity and subtlety of effective and reflective teaching.

The chapters within the book are linked by common themes: the principles of the reflective practitioner model are an essential element and are outlined in some detail in Ashcroft and Palacio (1995 and 1997). These principles include the need to look at issues of equality. Inclusivity and the dilemmas raised for the reflective teacher working within a largely constrained curriculum context are important foci for discussion.

The chapters raise the problematic nature of much of our 'taken for granted' knowledge about the curriculum. They look at intended as well as unintended consequences of action, and the need for teachers to remain open-minded and responsible. Open-mindedness implies that the reader neither rejects nor accepts the accepted orthodoxies about teaching and curriculum, but rather seeks to test ideas against the reality of their classroom and the available and emerging research and other evidence. The authors stress that this is not an objective and value-free process. The reader will be confronted with issues of responsibility: the need to consider ethical issues and the long-term as well as the immediate consequences of action. In particular, readers will be asked to look beyond a utilitarian stance, beyond 'what works', in order to look at the role of values in teaching and learning.

The authors present a view of reflective practice as an evaluation-led activity, that requires the collection of evidence about teaching, learning, assessment, values, beliefs and behaviour. This analysis is located within a moral, spiritual, social and cultural context. The meanings and experience of the various parties to the educational process are carefully considered.

The book also deals with the more immediate challenges that confront teachers in today's classrooms, including information and communicative technologies: their use and the issues they raise. In dealing with these issues the stress is on creativity in teaching and learning and the ways that such creativity can illuminate possibilities and problems such as those of match, progression and differentiation in teaching and learning. Throughout, the focus is on the analysis of effective teaching and learning. Understanding effectiveness requires an exploration of meanings underpinning current debates (for example, notions such as 'basics' and 'standards'). In this discussion, the book also addresses the political agenda in which the teaching of the core curriculum takes place.

A reflective approach to these issues leads to a focus on dilemmas rather than simple answers. This can be frustrating for new teachers looking for simple prescriptions for the problems that they face. We hope that the use of Case Study material describing the ways that real-life teachers have tackled some of these dilemmas, their successes and failures, will help to bring the issues alive. Although there can be few 'tips', the inclusion of knowledge-base for action, together with suggested sources for extending knowledge-base beyond that possible within the scope of the book, should leave the reader in a position to make better and more informed decisions within their particular context. Such decisions are always context specific: there are many simple educational questions, but we are increasingly certain that there are no simple answers. For this reason, authors have tried to locate the content and tasks within a theoretical framework. This framework is essential to inform action and decision making in a range of contexts.

This book is about the core curriculum in primary schools. It is not intended to be a guide or a set of tips and hints for all aspects of the core. The writers have tried to focus on how important aspects of the core subjects have developed since the introduction of the National Literacy Strategy and the announcement of the intention to introduce the National Numeracy Strategy in 1999/2000. At the time of writing the Qualifications and Curriculum Authority (QCA) had also published a syllabus for the teaching of science. All in all, the book was written at a point at which radical changes were being made, not in the content of the curriculum, but how the curriculum should be taught. For the first time since 1944 teachers were being expected to follow a prescribed pedagogy.

While the later chapters consider an aspect or aspects of the pedagogy of one of the core subjects, the first two chapters consider general ideas about the curriculum and about teaching and learning. All of the writers have borne in mind some of these ideas when they consider how teachers engage in the task of creating an understanding in pupils not merely of a particular subject, but how common sense and formal school knowledge differ.

Each of the subject chapters uses illustrative Case Study material to indicate innovative, and we hope, good practice. The Case Studies have also been chosen to show how teachers can respond creatively to recent pedagogical prescriptions and recommendations. In the case of English the writers examine ideas about teaching grammar, tackling the National Literacy Hour creatively and aspects of teaching genres. The two chapters on mathematics offer an introduction to and a critique of some of the ideas informing the National Numeracy Strategy. Finally, the chapters on science use Case Studies to show how primary school children can be taught to think and work as scientists.

References

ASHLEY, M. (ed.) (1999) *Improving Teaching and Learning in the Humanities*, London: Falmer Press.

ASHCROFT, K. and PALACIO, D. (eds) (1995) *The Primary Teacher's Guide to the New National Curriculum*, London: Falmer Press.

ASHCROFT, K. and PALACIO, D. (eds) (1997) *Implementing the Primary Curriculum*, London: Falmer Press.

KEAR, M. and CALLAWAY, G. (eds) (2000) *Improving Teaching and Learning in the Arts*, London: Falmer Press.

Chapter 1

Common sense and scientific sense
John Lee

Kenneth Baker was one the earliest users of the term 'core' in the context of the National Curriculum. However, the term 'basic subjects' or 'the basics' had already been in common parlance at this time. In recent years we have seen a swing back to the term basics to cover literacy and numeracy, but Kenneth Baker's core curriculum included science, and the recent emphasis by this government on ICT arguably makes it part of the core. It is not irrelevant to worry about what terms we use. When we talk about basic subjects we are saying that these are subjects that incorporate the skills and knowledge essential for success in school and later life. The idea of a core leads us to consider a body of knowledge and skills that will be shared by all pupils and in some way be at the centre of the school curriculum. We might argue that use of the term 'basic' leads us to see primary education not as a distinct but necessary stage in the pupils' school life, but as the elementary building blocks on which future schooling depends. In this second sense primary education becomes a preparation for the much more significant secondary stage. This sort of idea is encapsulated in the notion of elementary and secondary education, the terms used in England and Wales until 1944. In short, the arguments that led to identification of English, mathematics and science as core subjects are subtle and varied.

Enquiry task I

How can science be justified as a core subject if the arguments for English and mathematics are that these subjects provide the skills needed for learning all other subjects?

Make a list of the things taught in your school and identify them in the following manner;

Subject/area of knowledge	Essential for everyday life	Necessary for a decent job/life style	Essential for higher level learning

---

The idea that there is an essential core curriculum now seems like common sense but is it? We need to remind ourselves that a different core curriculum could be constructed. It all depends on what we decide is significant and important. Not so long ago very different ideas of what the core of the primary curriculum should be was current. In 1963 Sybil Marshall in *An Experiment in Education* described her work in a small rural school. Her focus is not subjects but the way children learn and how they represent things.

 Those who regret the wholesale instruction methods of their own schooldays, no doubt regret the lack of the bedside manner of the modern physician. They would be better employed spending their time thanking God that there is less and less need for either. (Marshall, 1963)

As you can see, Sybil Marshall had little time for whole class teaching. Nor did she think subjects needed to be taught separately. She argued that the best learning comes from the children and that children learn best through the expressive arts. In fact she went beyond this and was totally dismissive of fixed subjects and fixed timetables.

 No one has the right to shut the delight of English Literature up in a forty minute box, anyway, and to know that Hymn Practice has willy-nilly, to last forty minutes because the timetable says so is enough to make any child consign any and every hymn writer to perdition. (Marshall, op. cit.)

This diversion to the recent past should remind us that both the idea of a core, and the core subjects themselves are constructed by people, not fixed and given. This is usually referred to as the social construction of knowledge.

How is a core subject constructed?

If you look at the National Curriculum documents for English, mathematics and science you will see that what counts as knowledge of these subjects is laid out in the programmes of study. It is easy to forget that this document was fought over by a variety of groups of people, each group with its own interests. In other words, the core subjects of the National Curriculum were fought over, and subjected to revision in the wake of the Dearing Report.

Enquiry task 2

Compare the way that the content of mathematics, science and English are set out in the original curriculum documents and the 1995 revision.

You can see from this that in the case of mathematics and science in particular the way that the content is organised has been radically changed.

Why do you think this has come about?

In what sense are primary mathematics and science different now from 1998?

Each of the core subjects exists not just as core subjects of the school curriculum but also as subjects of study in universities and colleges. If we look at each in turn we can see how they have been constructed, more important we can show how they are often the sites of fierce disputes. It is easy to think that the content of these subjects and how they should be studied is a matter of common agreement but this is not the case.

English provides the clearest example of how subjects are fought over by various interest groups. Often people refer to the past, when it is claimed the content of English was well established. Students of English studied the classics of English literature: Chaucer, Shakespeare, Swift, Wordsworth and Dickens, for instance. Of course this ignores the fact that English is really quite a new university subject. It came into the universities only at the end of the nineteenth century, and in Oxford was considered to be rather too easy so all students were made to study Anglo-Saxon. If we look at the course in English on offer in universities and colleges today we can see a bewildering variety of content. Students may study a traditional course organised on chronological lines, *Beowulf* to Virginia Woolf, or study contemporary popular literature including Batman comics. It is little wonder that there is such a fierce dispute about the content of National Curriculum English when those who study the subject at higher levels are unable to agree on its nature. A good example of the way in which there is no easy agreement about English can be culled from school. I can remember tremendous staffroom battles over whether it was proper to allow children to read comics. Generally it was felt they were acceptable at playtime but not during class time, although for many children they were the one thing they read with enthusiasm and enjoyment. You might like to consider why Enid Blyton has been the subject of constant criticism from some teachers and librarians, not just on the grounds of sexism, but on the grounds that it is not real literature.

While it might appear that mathematics is more securely fixed, that there is a common agreement about its content and methods, this is not the case. Consider this story, a true one. A publican of my acquaintance employs students as part-time bar staff. He finds them pleasant and quick to learn but he says they cannot add and subtract in their head. What do you teach them now in school, he asks? Surely a student at a university should be able to add the price of a few drinks quickly and accurately and give the correct change? My acquaintance holds a view about the essential nature of mathematics that is not uncommon. However mathematics is not simply about arithmetic, it is about much more than this. In fact mathematicians study a wide variety of things many of which have little direct relevance to everyday life. Producing a proof of Fermat's last theorem will not help us to add the price of a round of drinks or give the correct change but it is clearly mathematics. Recently we have been told that pupils in England are not as successful in mathematics as pupils in the Pacific Rim countries. The press and politicians have argued that it is the neglect of particular aspects of mathematics that has caused this. What is happening is that mathematics is being constructed as knowledge and skills with numbers. Successful child mathematicians are not those who can solve mathematical problems but manipulate numbers to solve problems set by the commercial world. What we can see is that mathematics is being constructed as a much more restricted subject by the National Numeracy Strategy which will be discussed in detail in a later chapter.

Science is usually thought of as objective and neutral. In the public eye and in the eye of the child, scientists are seen as cold ratiocinators. Our students often ask school children to describe a scientist and their views are surprisingly like those that appear in popular fiction. A white-coated unemotional male working with mysterious apparatus. How can science be socially constructed? Surely it deals with the laws of nature and proceeds in a fixed manner? Really nothing could be further from the truth. One way to define scientific knowledge is to describe it as the result of what scientists do. In the past, for instance, there was one subject – chemistry – now we have organic and inorganic chemistry, colour chemistry, the chemistry of living things, biochemistry and so on.

It might be better to define science as methods and procedures connected to the creation of theories. When children really engage in science they do all of these things. I can illustrate this with an anecdote. A student was telling some Year 3 children the story of Noah's Ark and she used some pictures to help her. In one of the pictures the ark was shown floating and because of the way the picture had been drawn the water appeared to be curved. The children argued that the earth could not be round because the water would fall off, but in the end accepted that it was on the evidence of pictures from outer space. In scientific terms, they treated that as adequate evidence. More problematic was how the water stayed fixed on a sphere and they came to the conclusion that somehow the earth sucked. What the children had done was generate a theory by analogy from the evidence they had. Such work does not fit easily a view that science is somehow fixed and immutable knowledge to be acquired.

Enquiry task 3

Compare children's explanations of natural phenomena with the simplified explanations offered in children's scientific textbooks.

For instance you might ask:
- why do things fall to the ground when we drop them?
- why don't objects rise when they are dropped?

Compare their answers with simple textbook explanations.

Which are the most profound?

Common sense, science and knowledge

In the first part of this chapter we have shown that, rather than being fixed and immutable, the core subjects are socially constructed. However we do not mean that anything can be labelled as science or mathematics, only that the content of these subjects changes over time, and is somewhat dependent on the beliefs people hold. In this section we consider a model of what and how things can be learnt. In doing this we draw on some well known ideas.

There used to be an apocryphal character, the man on the Clapham omnibus, who was appealed to as a fount of ordinary wisdom and knowledge. What lies behind this is the idea that there is a common sense that cuts through jargon and academic specialism and reveals the world as it really is. It is a very attractive notion, but is deeply flawed. In fact common sense is often not sense at all. On many occasions common sense is just plain wrong or, worse, simply an expression of deeply held prejudicial views. Let us look at some examples to illustrate this.

In the case of English almost everybody has a view about the nature and purpose of grammar. At one point it was seriously suggested that teachers should spend time correcting children's use of English in the playground as well as in the classroom. What underpinned this risible notion was and is the idea that grammar is a set of prescriptive rules that can be applied in all circumstances. These deeply held common-sense ideas about correctness, and any deviation from this borders on the 'criminal'. In fact it is based on ignorance of language study and of the nature of grammar. In addition common sense usually mixes up aspects of pronunciation with grammar. We regularly hear that children's language is slovenly, that for instance they use the double negative. Sentences such as 'I didn't do nothing', are picked out as examples of this. Our man on the Clapham omnibus when asked to explain why this is incorrect will often say that two negatives make a positive and therefore what the child says is contradictory. The two negatives rule comes not from English grammar but from mathematics. In fact nobody is confused or believes that the child means to say she or he did something. In a similar manner the dropped 'h' is picked on as an aspect of slovenly speech, whereas the absence of 'h', the aspirant, is a feature of most English speech as is the use of the double negative. In these examples common sense may be damaging, in that judgments are being made about an individual's speech: something at the core of their self-esteem. Michael Halliday, the distinguished professor of linguistics, reminds us that the phrase 'I don't like your vowels' really means 'I don't like your values'. What Michael Halliday is pointing out here is that what appear to be linguistic, scientific judgments are not that at all. Most often they are judgments about an individual's social status. This is particularly evident in common sense judgments of pronunciation, as in the case of 'dropped "h"' or the use of broad open vowels such that 'soot', 'book' and 'cook' all rhyme. George Bernard Shaw notes in his preface to the play *Pygmalion* that no Englishman can open his mouth without revealing his social class and origins.

So the confusion about the double negative and the dropped 'h' is direct reflection of the way our society is divided along class lines. The use of the 'h' is a feature of what is often called with equal prejudice 'posh' speech. In like manner those who have spent the longest time in education will try to avoid the use of the double negative. Grammar is not a set of prescriptive rules, it is a formal scientific way of describing a language or language variety. The grammarian will be very careful to try to describe how people actually use language and will avoid setting down an ideal.

A final important point must be made here and it is that language changes. What was common usage 50 years ago is no longer the case now. A good example of this is the word 'decimate', which used to mean the destruction of 10 per cent of a population, but is now used to mean wholesale destruction.

We can see similar examples of errors and misconceptions in science and mathematics. In the past people held scientific theories and explanations that we would now think are laughable. The great naturalist, Gilbert White, one of the first to make careful scientific descriptions of English nature, was convinced that swallows hibernated in the mud at the bottom and edges of ponds. It seems strange that such a creative and intelligent man could be so wrong, but what he did was make a connection between the departure of swallows and his observation that a tortoise in his garden dug a hole in which to hibernate for the winter. It was simply common sense. We still make such unscientific assumptions. You might try asking both your colleagues and the children you teach to explain why lead is heavier than feathers. Mathematics is usually thought of as being concerned with complete accuracy but if that were the case no one would have been able to do the calculations enabling engineers to design a space rocket. When faced with a realm of mathematics where simple accuracy is not prioritised we are often bewildered. Think of the phrase, 'lies, damned lies and statistics'. This reflects a view that mathematics ought to be about total accuracy, while statistics tries to inform us what are the best chances of an event happening. Statistically I know that there is a strong chance that if I smoke it will lead to certain diseases but that does not mean that if I smoke I will definitely get a heart attack. Probability is difficult and seems not to be mathematical; after all it is common sense that if we do all those difficult calculations we must get accuracy.

If adults have misconceptions about the nature of knowledge it is fairly obvious that children will do as well. It is possible to overcome misconceptions by focusing *not* on common sense but on scientific knowledge. We are using the term scientific here as a counterweight to common sense: a scientific outlook is one that seeks for evidence to support opinions, descriptions and theories, and tries to avoid prejudicial statements. The model we have of learning and teaching shows how this can be visualised (see Figure 1.1). When children enter school they have a great deal

FIG 1.1
Moving from common
sense to science

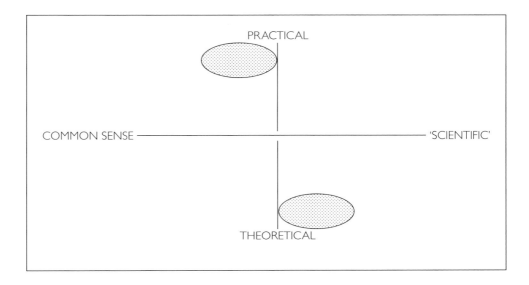

of practical knowledge. They also make sense of the world in their
own, and often very interesting ways. What we try to do in school is move
children from their own personal common-sense views of the world towards
a shared scientific one. Our diagram shows this as movement from the left to
right and from the top left to the bottom right. Work conducted in primary
science is a good example of this. Children are challenged to investigate why
things float and sink and to test fairly for the reasons they give. In doing this
we are not ruling out children's own explanations or thoughts. I can
illustrate the way children become scientific in the following way.

One of the scientific tasks set for the first SATs involved children in
predicting which objects would float and sink, and asked them to give
explanations. In one classroom I visited on the Friday afternoon after a
whole week of tasks a 7-year-old girl was asked whether an orange would
float or sink. She predicted it would float. When she tested out her
prediction the orange sank. When asked to revise her opinion she declared
it ought to float as she had observed during the week that oranges floated.
This may seem trivial but in fact this 7-year-old behaved in a profoundly
scientific manner. She refused to let the one instance of sinking override the
overwhelming evidence of floating she had observed all week. It is this kind
of thing we mean when we talk about a move from common sense to science.

Gilbert Ryle introduced an important distinction between two sorts of
knowing, and this distinction is also drawn on in our model of learning and
teaching. Ryle talks about a difference between 'knowing that' and 'knowing

how'. 'Knowing that' is rather like knowing the rules of a game or a set of facts about something. Ryle uses the example of someone learning chess, they may know the rules and be able to recite them but not be able to play competently. Once the learner knows the game they may forget the rules, they become part of the action of playing. Ryle is not dismissing 'knowing that' but makes the powerful point that we can do things competently without necessarily being able to make what we are doing explicit. He argues that people argue logically without knowing the rules of logic. Commenting on how people discuss and argue he says;

> *They do not plan their arguments before constructing them. Indeed if they had to plan what they think before thinking they would never think at all; for this planning would in itself be unplanned.* (Ryle, 1963)

On the vertical axis of our model we have placed the 'practical' and 'theoretical'. We do not mean by theoretical simply 'knowing that' but an ability to demonstrate understanding. Ryle makes the point this way;

> *Understanding is part of knowing how. The knowledge that is required for understanding intelligent performances of a specific kind is some degree of competencies in performances of that kind.* (Ryle, op. cit.)

The case of children understanding grammatical concepts or scientific concepts is dependent on them being able to 'do' grammar and to 'do' science. Simply giving them the rules or the facts will not inculcate understanding, which is what we as teachers are striving for.

Where have we got to?

We have argued that the idea of a core curriculum or of basics is contentious. That although it looks like common sense, it is someone's common sense. In other words common sense is less common than is often supposed. The content of the subjects English, mathematics and science is not fixed but is a social construct and the content of them can and does change over time. Often the prescription of content is a matter of prejudice rather than science. It is important, then, to move children from common-sense notions of knowledge and towards ideas based on reasoning and evidence. On the whole what we should be focusing on is 'knowing how' because that way understanding lies. In the case of an emphasis on 'knowing how' the Royal Society of Arts (RSA) in its advice to the Secretary of State during the debates about the emergent National Curriculum makes two important points about which we agree. The first relates to the division of the curriculum into conventional subjects and the idea of a core. The second emphasises the importance of 'knowing how' rather than merely 'knowing that'.

 Historical divisions of subjects do not necessarily provide a satisfactory way of describing curriculum needs for the future, given the rapid change in society. There is a danger that such an approach will accentuate an emphasis on knowledge itself rather than upon its applications. (in Haviland, 1988)

References

HAVILAND, J. (1988) *Take Care, Mr Baker*, London: Fourth Estate.

MARSHALL, S. (1963) *An Experiment in Education*, London: Cambridge University Press.

RYLE, G. (1963) *The Concept of Mind*, Harmondsworth: Penguin.

<table>
<tr><td>Chapter 2</td><td>Developing a core curriculum</td></tr>
</table>

Chapter 2 — Developing a core curriculum

John Lee

The surveys of secondary and primary education conducted by Her Majesty's Inspectorate (HMI) and published in 1978 and 1979 (HMI, 1978, 1979) respectively, signalled a major concern. The curricula of both primary and secondary schools were too varied and lacked breadth and balance. In the case of primary schools too much time was spent on English and mathematics to the detriment of what we now call the foundation subjects. HMI reported an absence of history and geography and rather scant attention to science and art and music. Topic or thematic work was done in most schools but this was often poorly planned, repetitive and lacked rigour. In brief, although most primary schools did some topic work and many teachers espoused a belief in independent and exploratory learning, primary schools were still in the grip of the 'elementary curriculum'. These studies can be seen as marking the beginning of an educational debate that eventually led to the introduction of the National Curriculum by the 1988 Education Reform Act (ERA). HMI were influential in promoting this debate and published from 1984 onwards a series of pamphlets entitled 'Curriculum Matters' which sketched out the range of subjects that were to become the National Curriculum.

The argument for the National Curriculum was based on three significant concepts, *breadth*, *balance* and *entitlement*. In the first case it was argued that the primary curriculum was too narrow. Children spent too much time on the basic subjects, English and mathematics. Other subjects were not taught systematically, coverage was sporadic and children's experience of subjects other than English and mathematics was far too dependent on the predilections of their teachers. The curriculum they experienced lacked balance, in that a range of subjects from the arts, humanities and sciences were not covered. It was also argued that insufficient attention had been paid to science, design and technology and information technologies. These subjects were identified as crucial. Finally the introduction of a legally binding National Curriculum ensured that all pupils would receive their entitlement to a broad and balanced curriculum.

Enquiry task 1

Find a description of the curriculum of your school before 1980 and compare it with the school's return of curriculum coverage given on the Pre-inspection Schedule of Information.

How does the pre 1980 curriculum differ from the account given in the Pre-inspection Schedule of Information?

How do these differ from the account given in the Pre-inspection Schedule of Information?

When the National Curriculum was first introduced it was the opinion of many teachers that it would lead to a reduction in the number of hours spent on the teaching of literacy and numeracy. However studies of the balance between 'basic' subjects and the rest of the curriculum show a remarkable consistency over time. Jim Campbell and his colleagues (Campbell and Neill, 1994) in a major study conducted after the advent of the National Curriculum found that the amount of time spent on basic subjects, English and mathematics, was very similar to that found in pre-National Curriculum surveys. It will be interesting to ask yourself whether this is the case in your school.

The rejection of a pedagogy

When Kenneth Baker, then Secretary of State for Education, introduced the ERA Bill in the House of Commons, 1 December 1987, he made it clear that while the government would determine the content of the curriculum it would not determine how teachers would teach.

After religious education come the three core subjects of English, maths and science, and seven other foundation subjects – history, geography, technology in all its aspects, a foreign language in secondary schools, music, art and physical education. In Wales, Welsh will have a firm place in the curriculum. We do not intend to lay down either on the face of the Bill or in any secondary legislation, the percentage of time to be spent on different subjects. . . . We want to build on the professionalism of the many fine and dedicated teachers throughout our education system. The National Curriculum **will provide scope for imaginative approaches developed by our teachers**.

(our emphasis) (in Haviland, 1988)

Mr Baker expressed, I think, a commonly held opinion that English and maths were the basics or building blocks of the curriculum. But he added to these science, which he argued was equally essential for a modern education. What he was also saying was that how subjects should be taught was a matter for teachers.

When Kenneth Baker described English, mathematics and science as core subjects he was giving them a more important status than the other subjects and this has had consequences. Schools felt they had to prioritise the teaching of these subjects but found difficulties in treating science in the same way as mathematics and English. Anecdotal evidence and the evidence of OFSTED inspection reports shows almost all primary schools teaching English and mathematics every day but focusing on science for blocks of time, often using content of science as an integrative theme.

The introduction of the National Curriculum produced many challenges for schools and teachers. Key Stage 1 teachers were faced with the task of turning the lengthy and wordy National Curriculum documents into practice. In doing this many believed that they were changing both what they taught, how they taught it and the amount of time they spent on each subject. Jim Campbell had this to say in the matter when he spoke at an invitation conference 'Developing the primary school curriculum: the next steps', organised by the School Curriculum and Assessment Authority (SCA) in June 1997:

> *Research by Alexander, Willcock and Nelson (1995); Campbell and Neill (1994a, 1994b; and Plewis and Veltman (1996) provides a general picture of continuity with previous practice rather than change, whether the unit of analysis is pedagogy and classroom discourse, time spent on subjects, integration of subjects or time spent on mathematics. This picture, of the primary curriculum being highly resistant to planned change, is not supported by all cognate research, notably the PACE project at Bristol (Pollard et al., 1994), but is congruent with most studies of curriculum development in the UK and USA since the 1960s, 1970s and 1980s.* (Campbell, in SCAA, 1997)

What Jim Campbell is saying is that for all the changes since 1988, for all the hard work of teachers, things have not really changed. Do you agree? Some of you will be in a position to see whether you have evidence to support this argument by doing something similar to Enquiry task 2.

Enquiry task 2

Find out how you planned work in English, mathematics and science just before the introduction of the National Curriculum in 1988.

How many hours were spent on each subject?

Was the content of each subject planned progressively from year to year?

Did the school plan topics or themes to be covered at particular times so as to avoid repetition?

Is school planning different now?

Recent changes: towards a national pedagogy?

If we look at both the professional press and the popular press since the establishment of the National Curriculum we can see a fierce debate about standards and quality in education. A wide variety of commentators, particularly the teachers' associations, declared that the National Curriculum would not improve standards, rather it would lead to a decline in standards. Since 1989, the year that the National Curriculum was first introduced into schools, claims and counter claims for whether it has improved standards have been made. Few of these claims have drawn on objective evidence to support their contentions. It was and is standards in English and mathematics that are the main focus of attention. Although some consideration was given to performance in science, on the whole this was muted, and continues to be so.

Once the National Curriculum had 'worked' its way from Key Stage 1 through Key Stage 2 and Key Stage 3 the problem of complexity and curriculum overload was highlighted particularly by teachers. Under considerable political and professional pressure central government appointed Sir Ron Dearing to review the National Curriculum. The Dearing Report proposed a slimmed down curriculum, a simplification of the subject documentation and a promise that there would be a five year moratorium on change. Sir Ron Dearing's proud boast was that he had fitted all of the Key Stage 1 and Key Stage 2 documentation into a document one centimetre thick!

The School Curriculum and Assessment Council's monitoring of the schools' responses to the curriculum focused on the use of time for the teaching of mathematics and English. In 1997 the authority reported that schools were spending more time on the teaching of English and mathematics than the Dearing Report had recommended, as can be seen in the table below.

	English	Mathematics
Key Stage 1	27%	20%
Key Stage 2	23%	19%
Weekly hours totals	10.1	9.9
Average teaching time devoted to mathematics and English.		
Percentages and hours totals of actual teaching time.		

Enquiry task 3

In your school:

What percentage of time is given to mathematics, English and science?
- before the introduction of the National Literacy and Numeracy Strategies?
- after the introduction of the National Literacy and Numeracy Strategies?

If a broad and balanced curriculum is to be preserved and primary schools are not simply to replicate an elementary school curriculum the problem of raising standards cannot simply be a matter of the amount of time dedicated to subjects. You will have noticed that the figures above relate only to English and mathematics and leave out the other core subject, science. You might consider the effect of giving the same amount of time to science as the other two subjects.

Dr Nicholas Tate, chief executive of the Schools Curriculum and Assessment Authority, has made a point not dissimilar to Jim Campbell's. Referring to the time allocation given in the table above he has this to say,

 These time allocations are also comparable to, and sometimes in excess of, many of those found in countries whose achievements exceed ours. The comparable figures for Singapore, for mathematics, for example, are 19%–20%, and for Korea, 16%. All this suggests we will not solve our problems simply by tinkering with the amount of time we allocate to different curriculum areas. We will certainly not solve them by reducing the curriculum to little more than the basics. This would only have the effect of further widening the gap between us and some of our economic competitors and between state and independent schools at home. The focus instead – and this where the government is concentrating its efforts – needs to be on how to make the best use of the time available, thus on teaching methods. (Tate in QCA, see SCAA, 1997)

In just under 10 years government has moved from a position where teachers were to be responsible for pedagogy and a consequent acceptance of diversity to one in which pedagogy can be prescribed.

From content to pedagogy

Where does this take us? We began with the concerns that led to the implementation of the National Curriculum. This was underpinned by a belief that pupils must have a broad and balanced curriculum but how it should be taught was a matter for the teaching profession. Academic research looking at the way these reforms affected schools suggested that little had really changed, that what was being taught and how it was being taught remained the same. Most of these researchers took a critical stance to the curriculum. Government organisations responsible for monitoring the curriculum and considering whether standards were improving came to rather similar conclusions. What now needs to be looked at, in the case of two of the core subjects, is what the evidence is for making statements about standards.

There is a problem here. It is simple – that although we have SATs results we have no standard measures of achievement in mathematics and English from *before* the introduction of the National Curriculum. This problem is compounded by the fact that SATs have changed radically during the years of the operation of the National Curriculum. You can see this very clearly if you compare the SATs materials for 1992 with those for 1996 or 1997. You might ask whether the same thing is being tested. Even so, the evidence of SATs scores has been used to support changes in the National Curriculum and as we shall see later, powerful recommendations on how subjects should be taught.

Let us look at the SATs results for 1996 and 1997 in English and mathematics, beginning with English (Tables 2.1 and 2.2). The 1996 results are shown in brackets.

TABLE 2.1
Key Stage 1 % of pupils achieving level 2 in English: the expected standard for their age

	All pupils (%)	Boys (%)	Girls (%)
Reading	80% (78%)	75%	84%
Writing	80% (79%)	75%	85%
Spelling	62% (na)	56%	68%

TABLE 2.2
Key Stage 2 % of pupils
achieving level 4 in
English: the expected
standard for their age

	All pupils (%)	Boys (%)	Girls (%)
English	63% (57%)	57%	69%

On the basis of these figures, and claims that we do less well than some of our economic competitors, the government has proposed a National Strategy for the teaching of literacy. It has declared that in the year 2002 80 per cent will achieve the expected standard for their age: in the case of 7-year-olds, level 2 – in the case of 11-year-olds, level 4.

In looking at these figures you might be as puzzled as we are. It appears that on the whole except for spelling, pupils at the end of Key Stage 1 are at or very near the target of 80 per cent at level 2 by 2002. Is radical strategy altering school and classroom organisation actually needed?

Even at Key Stage 1 the problem seems to be the differential performance of boys and girls. This is not new. The 1993 OFSTED Report 'Boys and Girls and English' reviewed the research on the performance of boys and girls from before the National Curriculum and in its early years. APU reports in 1983 and 1988 showed girls out performing boys in writing and reading comprehension at age 11 and that the difference persisted at 15.

Enquiry task 4

Compare the performance of the pupils in your school in the English SATs.

Are they in line with the figures above?

If you identify an achievement problem is it at Key Stage 2 or both stages?

Does your PANDA indicate that your results are on line?

How do boys and girls perform in your class and your school?

The National Literacy Strategy, which is discussed in detail in Chapter 3, may cause major changes in school and classroom organisation and management. In the light of your school results do you think it is needed at Key Stage 1?

Let us now look at mathematics. Before turning to the SATs scores (Tables 2.3 and 2.4) it is worth noting that international comparisons in mathematics are much easier to make than in literacy. The trend appears to be from international comparative studies that at 13 English pupils perform less well

TABLE 2.3
Key Stage 1 % pupils achieving level 2 and level 3 in mathematics in the task test 1997. The expected standard for 7-year-olds is level 2.

All pupils (%)	Boys (%)	Girls (%)
84% (82%)	82% (81%)	85% (84%)

(1996 figures in brackets)

TABLE 2.4
Key Stage 2 % pupils achieving level 4 and above in mathematics in the task test 1997. The expected standard for 11-year-olds is level 4.

All pupils (%)	Boys (%)	Girls (%)
62% (54%)	63% (ns)	61% (ns)

(1996 figures in brackets)

in numeracy tasks but they are better in some aspects of mathematics, for instance data handling.

Before discussing these figures we need to remind ourselves that the task tests only cover some aspects of the mathematics curriculum. Even so there seems to be a similar pattern to the scores for literacy and you may wonder whether changing to a radically new way of teaching at Key Stage 1 is really necessary. The situation at Key Stage 2 is different. As with literacy, if the government's target of 80 per cent pupils meeting the standard of level 4 by 2002 is to be reached then a number of questions need to be asked. One you might consider is whether the current curriculum is too demanding or too broad for a substantial number of pupils.

Enquiry task 5

Compare the performance of the pupils in your school in the mathematics SATs.

Are they in line with the figures above?

If you identify an achievement problem is it at Key Stage 2 or both stages?

Does your PANDA indicate that your results are on line?

How do boys and girls perform in your class and your school?

If you teach a Key Stage 2 class compare your pupils' performance in different aspects of the mathematics curriculum.

Conclusion

We have considered how the curriculum has changed since its inception. More particularly we have seen how the government now feels able to tell teachers how to teach, not simply what to teach. We look in more detail at the changes in the teaching of literacy and numeracy later in this volume. You will have noted that although science is a core subject and was identified as such as early as 1988, it has not received the sort of attention that mathematics and English have. You may wonder why that is so?

Annotated reading list

HAVILAND, J. (1988) *Take Care, Mr Baker*, London: Fourth Estate.
This reminds us of the way the National Curriculum came about and what the debates of the time were.

SCHOOLS CURRICULUM and ASSESSMENT AUTHORITY (1997) *Developing the Primary School Curriculum: The Next Steps*, Hayes: SCAA.
A collection of invited papers addressing what the curriculum ought to be like in the future. It contains many thought-provoking suggestions.

References

ALEXANDER, R. (1995) *Versions of Primary Education*, London: Routledge.

APU (1989) 'Assessment Matters. No. 4 Language for Learning', A Summary Report on the 1988 APU Survey of Language Performance, London: SEAC.

CAMPBELL, R. J. (1993) 'A dream at conception: a nightmare at delivery', in CAMPBELL, R. J. (ed) *Breadth and Balance in the Primary Curriculum*, London: Falmer Press.

CAMPBELL, R. J. and NEILL, S. R. St J. (1994) *Curriculum Reform at Key Stage 1: Teacher Commitment and Policy Failure*, London: Longman.

GORMAN, J., BROOKS, G., WHITE, J., MACLURE, M. and KISPAL, A. (1987) *Language Performance in Schools: Review of APU Language Monitoring 1979–1983*, London: DES.

HAVILAND, J. (1988) *Take Care, Mr Baker*, London: Fourth Estate.

OFSTED (1993) *Boys and Girls and English*, London: OFSTED.

SCHOOLS CURRICULUM and ASSESSMENT AUTHORITY (1997) *Developing the Primary School Curriculum: The Next Steps*, Hayes, SCAA.

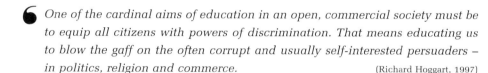

Chapter 3

The National Literacy Strategy: context and consequences

Helen Butcher

Introduction

> ❝ *One of the cardinal aims of education in an open, commercial society must be to equip all citizens with powers of discrimination. That means educating us to blow the gaff on the often corrupt and usually self-interested persuaders – in politics, religion and commerce.*
>
> (Richard Hoggart, 1997)

The imposition of a rigid framework using allotted portions of time to achieve specified learning objectives is a dramatic educational reform. More than just another bureaucratic paper mill, the form and content of the Literacy Strategy may change irrevocably the way we view teachers and teaching.

The history of the National Curriculum is one of passionate dispute by politicians and educators about curriculum content. In English the requirement to teach standard English and the importance of grammar have been sites of hotly contested battles (Brooks, Pugh and Hall, 1993; Cox, 1991). Pedagogy – the art of teaching and the decisions class teachers and headteachers make about how curriculum content will be taught – has until now remained the province of trained teachers. There is no precedent for one teaching method becoming a prescription for every classroom in England and Wales[1].

Although there were many misgivings about the introduction of the National Curriculum after the 1988 Education Reform Act, this did leave a great deal of space for the creativity and flair of individual teachers and schools. It also left scope for inconsistency and failure. The results of the Standard

Attainment Task for 11-year-olds in 1995 were the first indication of the disparity of achievement between schools. In response politicians traded some of the breadth, which characterised the National Curriculum, for an increased security about teaching of the 'basics'. The consequence of the decision to adopt the work of the National Literacy Project in all schools was the imposition of a 'top down' model on the teaching profession with less than two years' piloting and before an evaluation by the National Foundation for Educational Research (NFER) was published.

We must place the concerns of those who seek to improve the achievement of children in literacy against this background. There was almost universal agreement amongst teachers, parents and employers as well as politicians that this improvement was not only desirable but essential for pupils who will be adults in the twenty-first century. Ten years after the introduction of the National Curriculum, the investment of £59 million in the Literacy Strategy signalled a commitment to raise national levels of achievement in literacy towards the levels of success in literacy achieved by Finland, Norway, Italy and New Zealand.

Consider the following two comments about the Literacy Strategy that were voiced in the same staffroom in June 1998 just as national training for implementation of the Literacy Hour began.

> *What message does this send to our pupils and parents now we've got the Secretary of State writing our lesson plans?*

> *I wish this had been done sooner. All these years I've been deciding what to teach when and going to meetings about schemes of work that* didn't *work. Now the content and organisation has been decided I can get on with the bit I enjoy, which is* how *to teach the objectives to the children in my class.*

On the surface these comments appear to represent two ends of a spectrum of response to the Literacy Hour. Yet, I think they have more in common than a first reading suggests. The first speaker is suggesting that part of her skill as a trained professional has been to adapt curriculum content and teaching style to the requirements of each class she teaches. The second speaker also believes in adapting teaching to suit the needs of each class. Where they differ is that the second speaker is happy to concede organisational aspects of the teaching of reading in order to be able to concentrate on how to communicate learning objectives effectively to her pupils. Time previously spent deciding on 'what' and 'when' can now be devoted to differentiating her teaching for groups and individuals. The first teacher is convinced that decisions about what to teach and when are just as important to her pedagogy as decisions about how to teach it. The second teacher sees the allocation of an hour a day and suggested segmentation of the hour as a supportive framework within which a combination of her teaching skill and knowledge of the children can flourish. Unlike the first speaker she would argue that the *how* is still very much up to her, she still has to devise half-termly, weekly and daily plans.

This important debate features in different ways throughout this chapter which sets out to cover: the background to the development of the Literacy Hour; what a Literacy Hour comprises; the way it affects the work of teachers and student teachers; and the practical and pedagogical consequences which arise from this national programme. It is important to think about the impact of this new orthodoxy on pupils, teachers and whole schools. To help you gain some practical insight, each of the enquiry tasks focus on these different dimensions. The points for reflection are designed to develop your critical thinking specifically in relation to the Literacy Strategy. They should also develop your working knowledge of the document.

The case for action

The social and political context from which the National Literacy Strategy has emerged is concern about the standards of literacy, a debate with a long history.

 Too many boys and girls leaving the Secondary school show themselves deficient in ability to master the thought of a passage or chapter and to express their ideas in writing or orally with precision or clarity.   (Norwood Report, 1943)

It is interesting that each generation feels that literacy is their crusade and theirs alone. There is a conviction that standards are poorer than at any time in the past. Different commentators point to different times for the beginning of this debate: The Black Papers of Rhodes Boyson and Brian Cox (1975), James Callaghan's Great Debate (1978), or the recent (1997) study by Ivy Brember and Julie Davies suggesting that the impact of teaching 10 subjects in the National Curriculum to primary pupils may have resulted in poorer standards of literacy amongst 11-year-olds. Contention about whether to teach reading by starting with whole words or individual letters stretches back to the seventeenth century (Brooks et al., 1993; Morris, 1963).

During the 1980s interest in improving standards of literacy led teachers to consider fundamental issues such as motivation and purpose, for example, in

Reflection

Consider the following text for beginning readers printed in 1978. Each line corresponds to a page of the book, *Lad is a Dog*.

> Run Lad.
> Look Lad.
> See Lad.
> Jump Lad.

The accompanying pictures are ambiguous, there is no sense of a story or indeed any other purpose for wanting to read this. Looking at texts in your classroom how does the reading content differ from the text above?

one influential study Cox expressed the view that 'Reading is much more than the decoding of black marks on a page; it is a quest for meaning and one which requires the reader to be an active participant' (Cox, 1989).

Many people, teachers and others, came to believe that the way in which children were being taught was not in harmony with the way children learned to read and certainly did not inspire them to want to continue reading. That the way literacy is taught is an important factor in the achievement of sustained fluent reading was a central feature in the work of Don Holdaway (1979), Donald Graves (1983), and Kenneth Goodman (1987). Much of the time it seemed as if a sensation thirsty media sought to polarise the teaching profession into those who taught using phonics, an approach familiar to most journalists, and those who advocated what came to be termed 'real books'. The term 'real books' was coined to describe books made for reading to children that had strong narrative features. These were contrasted to books from reading schemes which, in their efforts to present text simply, often rendered reading meaningless.

A study carried out by Cato (1992) for NFER discovered only 4 per cent of teachers used 'real books' exclusively. The majority (68 per cent) used a combination of phonics – teaching a correspondence between sounds and letters, reading schemes, whole language approaches and 'real books'.

It is worthwhile reflecting that the same, often heated, debate polarising phonics and 'whole language' occurred in America and Australia, leading to major initiatives in both countries in the last 15 years. In America Marilyn Jager Adams (1990) was commissioned to survey the contemporary literature from all relevant fields to answer the question, what is the most effective way to teach reading? She concluded that phonological awareness is a vital skill in learning to read but

Reflection

Do you remember learning to read? Few adults who read well remember learning in any detail, whilst few adults who had difficulty forget.

If you can remember do you know whether you were taught using 'real books', mainly phonics teaching or reading schemes?

What is your intuitive belief about how children learn to read?

 to be most productive it [phonics teaching] may be best conceived as a support activity, carefully covered but largely subordinated to the reading and writing of connected text.

The subtleties of the debate about the importance of context in learning to read were overwhelmed by the Standard Attainment Task (SAT) results of 1995 which shook everyone with an interest in developing skilled readers. Less than half the 11-year-old school population (48 per cent) achieved the expected standards (National Curriculum level 4). Questions were asked by politicians, parents and commentators about whether the National Curriculum had failed the children it had been intended to support.

Gestation of National Literacy Strategy

Following publication of the SAT results for 1995, in January 1996 at The North of England Conference, Gillian Shephard, Conservative Secretary of State for Education, announced the creation of 10 Regional, and one National, Literacy Centres as part of a plan to improve basic skills. The regional centres were to work with about 20 primary schools for a period of two years, with the intention that this should be a rolling programme and by 2001 more than 2000 schools would have been involved.

In May 1996 David Blunkett, shadow education minister, established a Literacy Task Force chaired by Professor Michael Barber. The task force was charged with the responsibility for designing a strategy to ensure that, 'by the end of a second term of a Labour government all children leaving primary school will have a reading age of at least 11'. It published an initial report in February 1997 assertively titled 'A Reading Revolution' outlining the need for action – principally on the long tail of under-achievement in literacy across the country. National results for reading were in the middle band of countries alongside Germany, The Netherlands and Spain but showed evidence of lower ability pupils performing substantially below that of other countries.

In August 1997 following the election of a Labour government, the task force published its completed report entitled *The Implementation of the National Literacy Strategy*. In only five months they had moved from describing the need for action and outlining intentions to directing an initiative that would impact on almost every primary pupil and teacher in England and Wales.

Teaching reading: from autonomy to prescription

The implementation of the National Literacy Strategy is a *centralised* re-evaluation of part of the core curriculum. A political decision requiring schools to follow an explicit framework of teaching objectives using a prescribed pedagogy has usurped professional autonomy in favour of political pragmatism. There are two distinct strands to the development of the Strategy. One centres on content: exactly what do we mean by effective teaching of reading? In order to understand this we need to look at the context for the teaching of reading in the last 20 years. The other strand concerns form: how can we ensure that the teaching of reading is consistent and coherent within and between schools? These two inter-related strands can be described as the pedagogic and management aspects of the teaching of reading.

As recently as 1988, having responsibility for the literacy development of a class of primary school children meant class teachers decided what to teach, to whom, when and for how long, as well as the size and composition of groups. There were almost as many solutions about how to teach reading and writing skills as there were teachers. Work now called English, in the National Curriculum, was then described as language work. Providing the headteacher agreed her/his plans, a class teacher had great scope for developing a curriculum that met the needs of the children in her/his class.

Two examples from my own teaching spring to mind. The first concerned work on the topic 'Black and White' which led to a thorough investigation of newspapers – different stories and articles, different writing styles, different size print, with a class of 6 and 7-year-olds who finally produced their own newspaper – without a computer. Another class of 5 and 6-year-olds looked into the languages represented in the class and surveyed the similarities and differences in a range of simple words – hello, yes, no, mum, dad and numbers 1–10. These activities were designed to foster and develop the literacy skills – reading, writing, speaking and listening of each child – and their success lay in the shared enthusiasm for the project and for print. Success indicators for me were the active involvement of pupils who were not enthusiastic readers. Children who at other times would conveniently forget their 'reading' book were bringing into school scraps of paper on which they had written down words in their home language and translated them into English. There were no percentages of time allocated to different curriculum areas. A successful drama lesson – bringing alive a shared text such as *The Quangle Wangle Quee* by Edward Lear – was constrained only by the arrival of the next class or playtime. In common with most teachers, I placed great emphasis on teaching literacy and felt bewildered by media reports suggesting that teachers' efforts to make learning to read exciting and meaningful were not only misplaced but probably damaging.

Before the introduction of the National Curriculum, staff curriculum meetings discussed policy, coverage, progression and resources but generally stopped short of directly influencing pedagogical style. There were four main reasons why colleagues did not set out to impose teaching style: it would have presented a threat to the professionalism of colleagues; it was understood that teaching is a highly personal/contextualised activity; telling people how to do their job could easily prove counter-productive; and many teachers were busy trying to develop their own practice, conscious of the need to improve their own skills. These barriers to changing practice have been swept aside by plans for the Literacy Strategy.

Prior to the introduction of the National Curriculum, school inspection was organised differently and the local authority employed advisers whose job it was to help individual schools work with the opportunities and challenges they experienced. Their brief was guidance and support rather than inspection and criticism. Pupil achievement was measured by schools sometimes in conjunction with the local education authority.

This was the landscape in January 1989. Nine months later the ground had been cleared and the foundations laid for dramatic alterations. September 1989 saw the beginning of the National Curriculum and English, the only subject with its own capital letter, was one of the first binders produced. National training days introduced class teachers to *attainment targets* and *programmes of study*, the language of teaching was changing. To the relief of many teachers the National Curriculum binders did not jeopardise creativity nor tell them what to teach when. In fact in teachers' centres and other training sites across the country many teachers welcomed what they saw as endorsement of good practice in this first version of the English curriculum.

The curriculum was couched as an entitlement for all children and offered a range of experiences which teachers were required to provide for children at certain levels. The documents set out to indicate in broad terms what the English curriculum should comprise. Consequently the most effective way of realising National Curriculum aims was for schools to develop schemes of work which would ensure the delivery of this entitlement to the children for whom they had responsibility. Implementing National Curriculum requirements involved developing a school policy, knowing the children who came to a school, the teaching styles of members of staff and the resources available. The entitlement described in the National Curriculum was elucidated in individual school policies. This liberal approach was built on an understanding that learning takes place in a context: an understanding which in turn draws on the work of Vygotsky (1962), Bruner (1986), Wood (1998) who all identify the significance of time, place and language (culture) in our intellectual and social development. Their ideas, generally referred to as a social constructivist perspective, suggest that to decide centrally *when* to teach something is both inappropriate for children and deskilling for teachers (see also Chapter 1).

The introduction of the National Curriculum appeared to be revolutionary but largely affirmed best practice in relation to existing curriculum content. What changed was how children's work was described and planned. Where most Key Stage 1 children had experience of looking at leaves, fruits and seeds and insects (mini beasts) without specifically defining it as science, these now featured as Life and Living Processes in Science, Attainment Target 2. In English, changes centred on the explicit requirement to plan for speaking and listening, children writing for a range of purposes and the provision of a range of literature for children. For the first time there were national descriptions of the paths children should tread in order to reach expected levels of achievement by the end of each key stage.

Despite being very different from the National Strategy documents there are two ways in which the National Curriculum pre-figures the Strategy. The English National Curriculum separated out three elements in the teaching of English: Speaking and Listening; Reading; and Writing. Ten years later literacy skills have been broken into a further three strands: word, sentence, text levels. It is important to reflect that these subdivisions are imposed, not somehow 'natural'. The National Curriculum also indicates the range of knowledge and skills and expected levels of achievement of children in each year group. This is the second clear antecedent of the term by term format of the Strategy.

Many schools would argue that their policy for teaching English contributed to the unique flavour of their school, conveying values, priorities and intentions of the school. The counter argument is that the investment of time by schools particularising the National Curriculum for their circumstances could be spent more productively. Although each school is different, this argument runs, the goal of improved literacy is common to them all, making a national scheme imperative. Michael Barber of the Literacy Task Force (1997) stated,

 Bringing about a dramatic improvement in literacy standards is possible only if there is a consistent national strategic approach over a full parliament.

The Director of the National Literacy Strategy, John Stannard, articulated the benefits as efficient use of time, coherence and consistency and demonstrable progress. It is worth considering these claims separately.

Time

While the content of the literacy document intended to save schools spending precious time creating their own schemes of work, what was not made clear were the number of hours required to establish the effective operation of Literacy Hours. Staff training, school audits, target setting, purchasing and allocating resources, re-organising staffing and classes have all made huge time demands on schools.

Coherence and consistency

For some time the holy grail of primary and secondary education has been school effectiveness: what is it that makes some schools more successful at developing children's potential than others? In 1998 the Chief Inspector for Schools, Chris Woodhead, argued that difference in performance by schools is not accounted for simply by social disadvantage. Plenty of comfortably situated schools could be developing literacy skills more effectively just as some schools serving areas of serious disadvantage surpass average end-of-key-stage results. The view embedded in the Strategy is that greater control over the curriculum is one way of evening out differences in school performance. The advantage of a tightly specified curriculum for literacy is the opportunity for clear communication and a common understanding between, teachers, parents, schools and training institutions. The transition of children between classes and between schools is likely to be much smoother when it is clear what will have been covered (though not necessarily learned). Training courses, whether initial teacher education, continuing professional development, or training for support staff, will have a shared brief and common discussion points.

Demonstrable progress

That decisions have been made about when to teach what in English is unarguable, what will be argued about is whether the dissection and distribution are the most helpful way for children to be taught. You may wish to question the idea that all or even most children in their second term in Year 1 are ready to discriminate and identify 47 consonant blends. Similarly you might wonder why, 'look, cover, write, check' is not endorsed as a technique to help with spelling until Y3, although there are plenty of reception age pupils who use it in their second or third term. On the other hand the effort expended detailing teaching objectives in the *Strategy* makes the coverage of genre, syntax and semantics far more comprehensive than was common when they were left to either individual language co-ordinators or teams of staff (see Chapter 4 for more detail).

The nature of the prescription

Ten years after the introduction of the first National Curriculum another set of files was sent to schools. The content of the *National Literacy Strategy* framework heralded the end of autonomy in the teaching of reading in England and Wales. The question is whether they also represent the end of under-achievement.

The files contain a progressive programme for teaching reading set out in termly objectives for text, sentence and word level work. The National Literacy Strategy defines word level as work on phonics, spelling and vocabulary; sentence level as work about grammar and punctuation and text level covers comprehension and composition work. The language of teaching has been further modified and the model of teaching described above, interpretavist, flexible, broad, not always tightly focused, almost overturned. Instead of the opportunity to interpret the programmes of study there is term by term prescription. Class teachers transfer the objectives onto a planning pro forma for each half term indicating coverage of the word, sentence and text level objectives. They then use the medium term planner to draw up weekly plans which specify choice of text, details of organisation of groups and the supporting activities. The framework for the Literacy Hour uses 'teaching objective' as the vehicle for children's learning about print. The structure of the hour focuses intensively on the role of teacher, less so on the role of learner. One of the most interesting but as yet unanswered questions is whether or not this will alter learning outcomes. In other words, is this intense focus on a systematic description of content and timing sufficient to overcome the difficulties experienced by 40 per cent of children in learning to read. Some headteachers involved with the pilot claimed the impact of this tight organisation has had a clear impact on children's learning, one pointing to a 10 per cent rise in Standard Attainment Tasks results after a year with the project.

The structure of the Literacy Hour

Not only is the content specified term by term but the manner in which it is delivered is also prescribed. The objectives laid down in the file are taught during a daily session of one hour and that hour is segmented into four different elements. These are:

1   whole class teaching of text level work – comprehension and composition using a shared text;
2   whole class teaching of sentence and word level work – phonics, vocabulary, spelling;
3   independent working in ability groups on short activities designed to reinforce the teaching objectives and guided reading or writing;
4   a plenary session to reflect on the learning of the hour.

Each of these segments has a time budget.

Enquiry task I

This task considers pedagogy

Intention: to encourage reflection on a major development in curriculum specification. *This activity is enhanced if you work with a partner.*

Resources: paper, pen, partner

List the advantages of having a tightly specified curriculum for literacy.

List the disadvantages.

How important is it that the Literacy Hour has been designated as the way to teach the objectives in the Strategy?

Would the hour be more or less effective without the time budgets for each segment?

What might be the effect of sending the teaching objectives to schools as a scheme of work and allowing schools to decide when and how they would be taught?

Managing the teaching of reading

One of the most optimistic viewpoints about the Literacy Hour is that it will galvanise the huge amount of energy that has always been expended trying to raise standards of literacy in England and Wales. In 1996 the Literacy Trust knew of 900 different literacy initiatives including; *Books for Babies*; *Reading Recovery*, which was still being funded by some local authorities after government funding ended because of the high costs; *Bradford Better Reading Scheme*, a scaled down reading recovery which focused on children who had begun to read but were not making progress; Volunteer Reading Helpers, an organisation which trained volunteers to give extra intensive support to pupils.

Michael Barber made it clear that as much time and effort went into researching mechanisms required for effective change, as into the content of the Strategy file and training materials. The strategy builds on the work of Robert E. Slavin (1996) in America who developed a literacy programme called *Success for All*, the Australian literacy programme entitled *A Nation of Readers* and the New Zealand *National Literacy Project*. Put simply, the elements identified as necessary for successful change are consistent, sustained commitment by individuals and groups with different areas of responsibility. As a result training for the literacy hour began with three people who have different responsibilities in a school: the literacy co-ordinator (a classroom teacher), the headteacher and a governor with responsibility for literacy. Schools needed to make an audit of their current literacy provision and prioritise the use of distance learning materials that cover the area they identified as weakest in their school. Local education authorities provided a further tier of management with responsibility for helping meet the target. They became responsible for ensuring schools set challenging literacy targets and for monitoring the progress they make towards them.

One of the stated aims of the strategy was to ensure children have access to the most effective teaching methods. The strategy was designed to incorporate an appropriate balance of different styles or modes of teaching that in combination were intended to ensure effective learning. The different segments of the hour make different demands on teachers. The first two segments require a firm grasp of the teaching objectives, good exposition skills, sensitive questioning and the ability to sustain the interest of a large group of pupils. While this last characteristic is also required in the plenary session this segment of the hour is more heavily focused on the learner.

Enquiry task 2

This task focuses on *teaching* in the Literacy Hour

Intention: to investigate the range of teaching styles used within the Hour

Resources: Study Diary – allocate a section and date each Hour you observe

Note different teaching styles adopted during the Hour, how does the whole class teaching at the beginning of the Hour differ from the plenary?

Contrast the demands made on the teacher in the different portions of the Hour.

What are the different questioning techniques adopted by the teacher in guided reading?

See if you can observe different teachers and make a note of effective strategies for whole class and group teaching of reading.

Interview the teachers and ask if they feel there is more time to focus on teaching and learning now that decisions about when to teach and what to teach have been made.

Remember one of the concerns that led to the development of the Literacy Hour is the 'long tail of under-achievement'. For this task you are asked to focus on two children, one having difficulty with literacy and the other a child making average progress.

Enquiry task 3

This task focuses on *learning* in the Literacy Hour

Intention: to track the responses of 2 children throughout a Literacy Hour

Resources: Study Diary for recording observations

- During the whole class teaching observe where these children sit. Is it easy for them to see the text, including the bottom of the page?
- Would you say, by looking at their faces and where they have positioned themselves, that they enjoy this part of the day?
- How do they react when the teacher asks questions? Note body language, facial expression and any verbal response.
- Continue to observe these children when they are working independently noting exchanges with adults and other children, approach to the task set and strategies used when difficulties arise.
- During the plenary session note how well they are listening to other children reporting on their work. Try to determine whether they respond differently to this segment of whole class teaching from the opening segments.
- Look for indications that the children have understood the learning intentions (teaching objectives) and built on existing knowledge.

You may prefer to complete this task by looking at two separate Hours, observing one child at a time.

When you have completed the observations find a suitable time not long after the hour in which you observed the child to talk to her or him. Avoid direct questions such as, 'Do you like the Literacy Hour?', try to develop a dialogue connected to the text.

A new landscape

Pedagogical, practical and managerial features of the Literacy Hour are producing dramatic changes in classrooms. The experience of teaching is different, the experience of learning is different. Although a moratorium on changes to the National Curriculum had been declared by Ron Dearing in 1995, September 1998 saw a clutch of new initiatives all designed to focus schools on the core curriculum. The introduction of the Literacy Hour went hand in hand with the slimmed down curriculum. Baseline assessment for children in reception classes sought to establish the skills children arrived at school with. School literacy audits assessed areas of weakness which schools needed to address. Taken together these initiatives created a different terrain. Some common experiences amongst schools which piloted the National Literacy Project were significant changes in the following areas,

- organisation of the day
- listening to children read/parental concern
- teaching writing skills/word lists
- teaching phonics
- planning
- mixing paints

Each of these areas is given brief consideration below.

Reflection

To what extent is the Literacy Hour determining the structure of the school day in your school?

Organisation of the day

Some schools implemented the Numeracy Hour and Literacy Hour from September 1998 many teaching both Hours in the morning. If you are already familiar with primary schools you will know that an hour of literacy and an hour of numeracy as well as assembly and break time leaves very little space for any other work in the morning session. A fear voiced by some colleagues in school is that this will see a return to the 'skills and frills' pattern of a primary school day, certainly at Key Stage 1, in which the morning is devoted to matters of *significance* and the afternoon to areas of the curriculum deemed (by some) to be less important, such as role play, art, sand and water – 'drills and spills' might be more apt.

In order to accommodate this restructuring of the primary curriculum some schools moved their assemblies and PE sessions from morning to afternoon. Other schools had to consider whether to have the Literacy Hour running at the same time throughout the school or whether resource issues made this impossible. Many schools did not have enough additional adults or indeed enlarged texts to run the Hour concurrently for all classes.

Listening to children read

Fewer primary staffrooms reverberate to the anguished question, 'how do I hear them all read?' An arduous but cherished cornerstone of primary teaching has been the commitment to hearing children read individually on a regular basis, in some cases every day. This has been criticised as an inefficient use of valuable teacher time, particularly in cases where no *teaching* takes place, rather, reading is monitored. During individual reading the rest of the class are deprived of teacher availability while at the same time teacher and reader are subject to regular interruptions from children requiring attention: a highly unsatisfactory learning experience for all concerned. The Literacy Hour replaces listening to children read individually with a composite of three different reading experiences, **shared**, **guided** and **independent** reading.

Shared reading
Shared reading occurs during the whole class teaching at the beginning of the Literacy Hour. Using a text for the week the teacher models reading, demonstrating the range of cues that readers use to derive meaning from text. These are defined in the Strategy document as; knowledge of context, word recognition and graphic knowledge, grammatical knowledge and phonic knowledge. Using the relevant objectives for each term class teachers teach

features of text: for example genre, layout, blurb, plot, character development; features of words – phonemes, blends and letter strings – and features of sentences: grammar and punctuation.

Commentary

The strength of the learning experienced by these children lay in the class teacher's knowledge of relevant and related texts and her knowledge of what would appeal to this group of learners. The juxtaposition of the two texts meant there was a shared context, the very enjoyable story of Handa, in which to set their developing knowledge and interest in the origins of fruit. Not all the activities fitted into the Literacy Hour though all the activities fulfilled requirements of the Literacy Strategy. The high quality of the information selected for inclusion in *Eating the Alphabet* meant children added to their knowledge in ways which were memorable to them. Part of the description given for avocado pear is, 'The avocado grows on a tree that is native to Mexico and Central America. It is also called an alligator pear'. As a direct consequence of this explanation children pursued the location of Mexico and pictures of alligators.

Guided reading

In the structure of the Literacy Hour, during the 20 minute period in which pupils work in groups, the teacher is expected to take one group for guided reading. Where this works, children read, with a teacher acting as a guide, twice a week. In fact a number of pilot schools have found it impractical to undertake this with two groups in the allotted 20 minutes and only set out to guide one group. There are implications for pupils, teachers and parents from this aspect of the hour.

If they adhere strictly to the Strategy, pupils and teachers lose out on the close contact afforded by individual reading. However they may gain more than they lose. Demonstrating the social features of reading is good practice, and structuring part of their reading as a group experience reflects this. Sharing opinions, predictions, difficulties and returning to the text at the end of guided reading to re-read in pairs or in unison all help to challenge the idea that reading is an isolated and isolating experience. Guided reading also helps pupils understand that peers as well as teachers can help with learning to read. A teacher will have the opportunity to make explicit teaching points about the text and the inevitable duplication of advice and guidance will be reduced in a group setting.

Guided reading is a very specific and prescribed way of working with children to develop their reading skills. For the teacher guided reading involves: selecting a text which provides a challenge for each child in the ability group and marries with the teaching objectives for the whole class; setting the scene or introducing the book; preparing the text fully in order to be able to anticipate teaching points and relate them to the objectives for that week; deciding a focus – what needs to be introduced and what needs to be practised. Teachers need to be very knowledgeable about the texts they use with children. The next book in the reading scheme will frequently not be appropriate. Matching texts to a group so they meet the demand for it to be 'challenging' is a skill that evolves over time but is nevertheless taxing, especially for those who are not English specialists. However, knowing which book is good for which phoneme or consonant blend is less important than the ability to convey detailed understanding of and enthusiasm for the book as a whole.

Enquiry task 4

This activity focuses on guided reading

Intention: to undertake some guided reading

Resources: sufficient copies of the selected text for each child to have a copy

Key Stage 2
- Select a fiction text which provides a challenge for the 'middle' ability group in your class.
- Read and prepare the text, noting style, difficult vocabulary, the development of character and plot.
- Introduce the text and ask the children to help anticipate the story using the cover, illustrations and blurb.
- Invite the children to read the text to themselves.
- Move around talking to each of them about what they are reading, bearing in mind your preparatory work and the teaching objectives for the week.

Key Stage 1
- You may wish to create a story bag or box to support your chosen text – this means collecting props or images that relate directly or indirectly to the story and offer stimulus for discussion.
- Prepare a text as for Key Stage 2 (see above) adapting the reading of the text to your group. They may read aloud or you follow the text while you read.
- Remember you must return to the text when focusing on the teaching objectives.

Reflect on your learning from this experience and the learning of the children.

How would you improve your next guided reading session?

Parental concern

Some parents, and some Ministers of Education, when confronted by an infant classroom notice the paints, the sand and the role play area and wonder whether the children receive any formal instruction. In this respect early childhood educators in England and Wales have failed to communicate their values, beliefs and curriculum effectively. The existence of a material object, a reading book, which indicates at the very least a conversation with a teacher during the course of the day and hopefully suggests that they have 'been reading' can assume great importance to parents. Clear communication between schools and parents about adaptations to reading procedure is vital. Where **guided reading** curtails the common practice of sending books home with children, for example because all copies of books have been grouped together for use in school, parents need to know and they need to know why. Schools may need to put a lot of energy into talking to parents. During the early implementation of the Literacy Strategy one headteacher commented, 'at first parents thought by not listening to children individually we were letting their children down, but when the children started talking about the Literacy Hour, and books in general, with enthusiasm, they relaxed'.

Not all pilot schools stopped hearing children read individually. Some Key Stage 1 classes found children reading aloud in a group but at their own pace impractical and chose instead to hear each child read part of the text while the others listened. Even schools which adopted guided reading whole-heartedly reserved the right to target particular pupils for individual support. The practice of sending books home for reading with family members has altered. Some schools no longer send books home, others invite children and their carers to borrow from a range of books but do not undertake to monitor or log details of texts selected.

Independent reading

It is important that children still have planned opportunities for independent reading. Uninterrupted, sustained silent reading (USSR), which has other acronyms such as ERIC (Everyone reading in class), in which the whole class spend 15–30 minutes independently reading books they have chosen, has sometimes been substituted for teaching reading. The Literacy Hour addresses the need to continue to teach children about reading long after they have achieved fluency. However, teaching literacy well will require enrichment of the Hour in a range of different contexts: USSR still has a valuable place in the curriculum. Additional opportunities are library sessions, reading to younger children, reading plays and browsing in book corners. In these settings pupils will have the opportunity to read texts they have selected.

Case Study

Teaching writing skills

The objectives set out in the Literacy Strategy covered by this Case Study are Year 5, term 3; objectives 2, 3 reading comprehension and 7, writing composition.

A Year 5 class teacher working in a primary school surprised his class by beginning the week with the story of *The Gingerbread Man*. Before he did so he asked the children to take note of the structure of the story. As a way of developing a sense of audience and purpose he then invited his class to write stories for a Year 1 class in the school specifying that the story had to have a repeating refrain. The class teacher helped prepare the class by using a shared writing session to list traditional tales the children knew which included a repeating refrain. *The Three Little Pigs*, *The Three Bears*, *The Three Billy Goats Gruff* and *Jack and the Beanstalk* were written on the white board by the children and they began to discuss their own memories of hearing these stories as children and how they could remember joining in with the repeated section. One girl told how she read a simple version of *Jack and the Beanstalk* to her younger brother who despite being only two ran round the house saying, 'grind bones, make bread'.

During the independent activities a different group each day had to *collaborate and plan* the production of a story, meeting the specification. Each child within the group then had to select a character and write the story from their perspective. The teacher made it clear the 20 minute period during the Literacy Hour was for planning. There would be a whole afternoon the following week when they would have the opportunity to write the story.

One group of four simply retold the story of *The Gingerbread Man*, taking the perspective of the gingerbread, the old woman, the fox and the cow. Picking up the theme of three another group produced, *The Three Grumpy Caterpillars* with a jaunty refrain, 'Watch out minch munch munch, Watch out we're a hungry bunch', called out to different vegetation as the three approach.

An additional afternoon was required for polishing and presenting the finished stories before they proudly read and, in some cases, performed the stories to the younger children. The Year 1 children spontaneously demanded to write their own 'gingerbread' stories and the process was reversed a fortnight later, (Year 1, term 3, Text level work objectives 5, 6, 8 – reading comprehension, 13, 14 writing comprehension).

Commentary

The value of having a genuine audience for writing cannot be over-emphasised. Writing for younger children in the same school, or a paired school, is a tried and tested method of encouraging Key Stage 2 children to consider some of the compositional aspects of different genres. In this example two important details are worth commenting on, the use of collaboration in planning the story and the allocation of additional time for writing the story. Children who lack confidence with story writing gain a great deal of support from being encouraged to adapt the structure of a familiar genre and through sharing the compositional task.

Concern was expressed during the pilot project, by both Key Stage 1 and Key Stage 2 teachers, that the pace and subdivisions within the Literacy Hour did not allow the consideration and reflection required by the writing process.

A number of schools have built in extra opportunities for extended periods of writing. The experience of shared and guided writing is that of consistent and intensive support and builds on the work of Don Holdaway (1979), Nigel Hall (1987) and the Exel project co-ordinated by David Wray (1997). In the National Literacy Strategy Guided Writing involves teachers' explicit teaching about the multi-faceted task of writing. At word level children are taught the necessary grapho-phonic knowledge to write and spell confidently and taught handwriting in ways that make connections between writing and spelling. At sentence level pupils are taught the grammatical knowledge required to help make their meaning clear. At text level the conventions and processes involved in different genres are modelled and scaffolded. 'Teacher modelling of complex cognitive activities has emerged from our research as a teaching strategy of major importance' (Wray, 1998).

The National Literacy Strategy incorporates a great deal of contemporary understanding of genres – see Chapter 4. What is not clear is how children are to have the opportunity for extended writing. Children are expected to do two short activities during the group work segment of the hour, which means there is no opportunity for the reflection, organisation and production of any well-considered piece of writing. Schools need to find other times during the week in order to provide opportunities for pupils to give sustained consideration to the form of what they write, the audience they are addressing and the quality of their work.

Enquiry task 5

This activity is about grammar and genre exchange

Intention: to experience interesting ways of teaching grammar

Resources: paper – not exercise books

Sentence level work – Y6, term 2 grammatical awareness:

'consider how the passive voice can conceal the agent of a sentence'

Before embarking on this activity you need to have established trust and respect within the group.

You may wish to organise writing partners and develop a culture of commenting constructively on each others' work.
- Invite the class to write individual recounts of a 'surprising day' they have had recently.
- When they have completed the recount collect the work but do not mark or comment on it.
- In the next timetabled extended writing opportunity distribute the recounts to writing partners.
- Invite partners to rewrite the recount as a report using the passive voice.

Allow time to discuss as a whole group the challenge involved in concealing the 'agent'.
- Ask if they realised they were also 'exchanging genres' and explore other common genre swops e.g. notes from texts, historical accounts from original documents.

Word lists

The inclusion of word lists for pupils to learn by the end of reception and the end of Key Stage 1 is one of the most controversial aspects of the Strategy. 'Sight vocabulary' is a term used to describe high frequency words which children need to be able to read. Again, it pays no attention to context, in some schools pupils will easily exceed the list of 45 words to be read by the end of reception, in others achieving 20 will be evidence of solid and effective teaching on the part of the class teacher. Those with responsibility for the National Literacy Strategy point to schools which achieve very high levels of literacy with challenging pupils and argue that high expectations are the single most important factor in successful teaching. If the long tail of under-achievement is to be tackled some demanding targets are necessary.

The command written above the word lists in the Strategy document 'to be taught as sight recognition words' made some teachers anxious about a return to 'flash cards'. This was a technique where children had to read single words, printed on card, which were flashed at them without any meaningful context. The serious drawback with flashcards was that if pupils knew the word they weren't learning and if they didn't it was a very uncertain way of being taught. The words in the National Literacy Strategy document are selected because of the frequency with which they appear in print, they are **key words**. This means that reading the very simplest text requires the reader to know these words. Pupils need to be confident in their reading of key words if they are to progress to more sophisticated reading, *but* they may not become confident, enthusiastic or fluent readers if these words are drilled.

Enquiry task 6

This activity focuses on word level work

Intention: to examine the word lists and search for meaning

Resources: NLS Document, a library of high quality texts

Try to make sentences using the list of words for reception children.

You can add the names of children in the class or characters from folk tales or reading scheme books.

Try grouping the words together to make them interesting to teach and to learn.

Investigate enlarged texts suitable for reception children and note down titles in which some of the key words are prominent.

Try using *This is the Bear* by Sarah Hayes, a delightful rhythmical text with a strong story line.

In 1988 a survey of London infant schools *Young Children at School in the Inner City* (Tizard, Batchford and Plewis, 1988) suggested that the many average infant-age children were actually engaged with reading for no more than eight minutes a day. The Literacy Hour is in part a response to such findings as well as comparisons with other countries like New Zealand in which much more time is spent focusing on the teaching of reading. Increasing the amount of sustained time children spend engaging with print with the help of an expert guide (their teacher) has been an important intention of those designing the Strategy.

Teaching phonics

Peter Bryant and Usha Goswami (1990), Lyn Layton, Karen Deeny and Graham Upton (1997) amongst others have sought to intervene in the conflict between those promoting whole word recognition and context cueing and those defending a phonic approach to the teaching of reading. The work they have undertaken set out to establish whether there was a link between phonological awareness, that is the skills needed to analyse the sounds in spoken and written language, and reading success. The evidence they cite suggests a correlation between the ability to hear rhyme at an early age and fluent reading. Interestingly, while pointing to children's sophisticated skills in breaking words into their constituent parts all the above are convinced that this needs exploring in a meaningful context. Young children are encouraged to play with words in nursery rhymes, older children to look for analogy between words, for example, hand and sand. Analogy in the context of the Literacy Strategy has a specific definition, 'relating something known to something new . . . emphasis on analogy encourages learners to generalise existing knowledge to new situations'.

 Stories are central to the analogy process. The key words should be left echoing in children's heads.   (Usha Goswami, see Williams, 1997)

It is in large part due to the work of these writers that word level work with an emphasis on identifying phonemes, consonant blends, digraphs and trigraphs feature in the Strategy. The Strategy endorses the need for teaching this detailed word level work in context rather than by arid drilling and publishers have rushed to produce enlarged texts featuring stories, poems and rhymes that match the word level teaching objectives.

In Year 1 term two, the suggestion is that children are introduced to 47 different consonant clusters, initial clusters for example bl, gl, pl, spl and ending clusters such as nd, nk, nt, nch. They are expected to be able to discriminate, blend and spell all 47 by the end of their second term.

Planning

A class teacher,

 Planning the hour is an art form. At first it took me half of Sunday just to plan five hours of my week. Now the children are familiar with the structure I present similar type activities using different texts and the planning is much quicker. The best bit is sharing ideas with other members of staff.

The planning documents within the Strategy focus the content of the hour very tightly. Teachers can use the specified termly content to plan in the medium term and then on a weekly planning sheet which details the specific teaching objectives for each day and the activities the different ability groups will be working on each day to reinforce the teaching objectives. They also need to indicate how the plenary session will further strengthen the children's learning. The English curriculum co-ordinator of a pilot school emphasised the need for planning the plenary, 'teachers have to be careful not to return to the laxness of "show and tell" sessions', the plenary is not 'look what we've been doing' it is 'look what we've learnt', this only happens where the lesson is centred on the planned objectives.

Enquiry task 7

Activity: Planning to teach at text level

Use the enlarged text *Caterpillar Diary* (Drew, 1987) Thomas Nelson

Study the text level teaching objectives for reading comprehension and writing composition in non-fiction for Y1 term 3.

Using the main text and the chart on the back cover to plan how you would introduce and structure teaching to support children learning to, '*locate parts of text that give particular information including labelled diagrams and charts*'. (Teaching objective 19)

Consider ways in which you could use *Caterpillar Diary* in tandem with *The Very Hungry Caterpillar* (1974) by Eric Carle.

A careful examination of the chart will indicate an important factual error in Carle's book.

Invite children to collaborate on their own non-fiction texts considering the information they wish to present, and the order in which it should be presented.

Mixing paint

For the guided reading element to be successful the teacher must not be interrupted by queries from other children. Although the Literacy Hour is devised so that a class teacher can teach the hour without additional help there is no question that the provision of another adult helps the third segment of the hour to run more smoothly. Indeed OA (other adult) is printed on the planning sheet included in the Strategy document. Where pilot schools had existing non-teaching assistants many found their role altered from mixing paints and cutting paper to working with children supporting literacy activities. Although most non-teaching assistants had previously spent some time helping children, for some this was the first time they had been so intensively involved and carefully planned for. There are various consequences of this: it may enhance the esteem of non-teaching assistants but may result in the loss of work being done previously.

Non-teaching assistant,

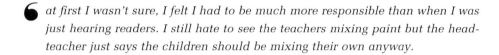 *at first I wasn't sure, I felt I had to be much more responsible than when I was just hearing readers. I still hate to see the teachers mixing paint but the head-teacher just says the children should be mixing their own anyway.*

Class teacher,

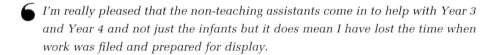 *I'm really pleased that the non-teaching assistants come in to help with Year 3 and Year 4 and not just the infants but it does mean I have lost the time when work was filed and prepared for display.*

Headteacher, (smiling):

we feel we have shot ourselves in the foot. Since being so involved in support-ing the Literacy Hour Mrs M has decided to become a teacher. She is starting an access course in September.

Conflicting evidence, oversights and questions to consider

Following the final report of the Literacy Task Force (August 1997) the Standard Attainment Task results for 1997 were published, indicating a clear improvement in the number of 11-year-olds reaching level 4. This improvement pre-dated the nation-wide Strategy. All of a sudden four years to increase national average scores by 17 per cent didn't look quite as ambitious.

	% of 11-year-olds achieving Level 4
1995	48%
1996	56%
1997	63%
1998	65%

A report commissioned by the Qualifications and Curriculum Authority (QCA) 1998 comparing the performance of French and British 9–11-year-olds indicated superior performance by British pupils in spelling, use of tenses and story writing. Fench pupils were better at using commas. 'The British emphasis on practice writing may be more effective than the French stress on structure and syntax' (Planel, Broadfoot, Osborn and Ward, 1998).

Early indications from the National Foundation for Educational Research suggested that:

 pupils participating in the National Literacy Project (1996–1998) who were entitled to free school meals made less significant progress than those not entitled. In many cases these are the very pupils in the target group.

The direction the Literacy Strategy takes us is away from entitlement (of pupils to a broad and balanced curriculum) towards enforcement (of teachers to teach what has been ordained).

It is interesting to consider the issue of entitlement in relation to the Literacy Hour. Almost every pupil in England and Wales will be taught the Literacy Hour but not all pupils have the same opportunity of access to the good features of shared and guided reading and writing. Pupils with hearing loss, pupils with English as an additional language, pupils who are exceptionally able or less able disrupt the attractive uniformity, the corporate image of the Strategy. It is true that guidance was issued by the National Literacy Strategy concerning each of these groups but it is significant, and in contrast with the National Curriculum, that it came after the documents and training materials had been published.

In summary, the National Literacy Strategy is a centrally devised and co-ordinated mission to improve standards of literacy. The immediate consequences of implementing the Literacy Hour are the alteration of the school day, intervention in the English curriculum, the organisation of children reading in school, and the deployment of non-teaching staff. The detailed mapping of term by term goals establishes a common language for teachers, pupils, parents and Institutes of Higher Education. The long term consequences will need to be considered not just in terms of the target set – the management component – but from a pedagogical perspective. David Reynolds (1998) comments on the lack of 'significant practitioner input' and wonders what may flow from this neglect, 'any clear absence of engagement by teachers in the educational process they are to be involved in from summer term 1998 may have damaging consequences on the reliability and implementation of "good practice"'. The way teachers respond to the challenges and dilemmas posed by the National Literacy Strategy will play a significant part in the way the Strategy evolves.

Failure in learning to read restricts and damages lives. We need to consider the following questions: who controls curriculum content and to what extent? What lessons about learning are we teaching children if a formula of exposition, activity and plenary, sometimes called training, is endorsed as **the** way to learn to read and to count? On the other hand can we continue to languish in the literacy 'B' team of developed nations? The demands made of readers are changing, the ability to skim and scan print, process text and make judgements quickly about its personal relevance and value are even more vital now than they ever have been. It is essential that the long tail of under-achievement is attacked. It may be that the intensity of the focus on literacy, rather than the particular pedagogy or allocation of time budgets, results in at least 80 per cent, hopefully more, 11-year-olds reaching level 4 or above in 2002. The test of the Literacy Hour will not be in 2002, but later, when these children are adults.

Note

1   In August 1997 the Welsh Inspectorate announced that adoption of the Literacy Hour by Welsh schools was a matter for 'local discretion'.

Annotated reading list

WRAY, D. and LEWIS, M. (1998) *Extending Literacy*, London: Routledge.
Wray and Lewis critique the notion that reading information texts involves 'higher order' or 'advanced' reading skills, they also challenge assumptions in the phrase 'information retrieval'. They argue 'children of all ages and abilities can become successful users of information texts'.

The authors offer clear guidance for helping develop children's non-fiction reading and writing with good illustrative examples. The book discusses the complexity of the task facing children when asked to write non-fiction. Wray and Lewis use Case Studies to demonstrate ways teachers can help move pupils from 'external' to 'internal' scaffolds. This book will help enhance 'text level' work in reading and writing non-fiction.

WYSE, D. (1998) *Primary Writing*, Buckingham: OUP.
Wyse offers a range of examples of children across the primary age range using the 'process approach' to writing. The importance of maintaining and developing what has been learned from Graves (1983), Holdaway (1979) and Goodman (1987) about acting as an experienced guide to the apprentice writer is emphasised and built on in this book. Read in conjunction with *Extending Literacy* this will provide a solid foundation for promoting high quality writing in children.

DEAN, G. (1998) *Challenging the Able Language User*, London: David Fulton and NACE.
Dean presents a very constructive and readable account of the tension created within the parent, child, teacher triangle when the child, is functioning at a significantly more advanced level than her or his peers. The book is full of extension activities and ideas for helping differentiating the English curriculum, and Literacy Hour, for able children. Many teachers recognise the need to make extra provision for sophisticated language users but are unsure about how to set about it. The Literacy Hour will pose particular difficulties, but this book will help with solutions.

HALL, N. and ROBINSON, A. (1996) *Learning About Punctuation*, London: Multilingual Matters.
Nigel Hall introduces this collection of articles commenting on the lack of writing about young children and punctuation. He also notes the lack of agreement by theoreticians on either definition or pedagogy. Chapter 2 covers invented punctuation illustrating how emerging writers convey meaning with their own attempts at punctuation. There are some entertaining and moving examples.
Anne Robinson talks to teachers about feelings and practice around the teaching and learning of punctuation. There is a detailed examination of the teaching of punctuation in one shared writing lesson.

LAYTON, L., DEENY, K. and UPTON, G. (1997) *Sound Practice: Phonological Awareness in the Classroom*, London: David Fulton.
A manual for developing children's phonological skills. The authors outline some of the relevant research and suggest a range of games and activities for extending children's phonological knowledge. Note activities on pp. 19–27.

References

ADAMS, M. J. (1990) *Beginning to Read*, Cambridge, MA: The MIT Press.

BAIN, R., FITZGERALD, B. and TAYLOR, M. (1992) *Looking into Language – Classroom Approaches to Knowledge About Language*, London: Hodder and Stoughton.

BOARD OF EDUCATION (1943) *Norwood Report*, London: HMSO.

BOYSON, R. and COX, B. (eds) (1975) *The Fight for Education*, London: Dent.

BREMBER, I. and DAVIES, J. (1997) 'Monitoring reading standards in year 6: a 7 year cross sectional study', *British Educational Research Journal*, **23**, 5; December 1997.

BROOKS, G., PUGH, A. K. and HALL, N. (1993) *Further Studies in the History of Reading*, Widnes: UKRA.

BROWNE, E. (1994) *Handa's Surprise*, London: Walker Books.

BRUNER, J. (1986) *Actual Minds, Possible Worlds*, Cambridge MA: Harvard University Press.

BRYANT, P. and GOSWAMI, U. (1990) *Phonological Skills and Learning to Read*, Hove: Lawrence Erlbaum Associates Ltd.

CARLE, E. (1974) *The Very Hungry Caterpillar*, London: Hamish Hamilton.

CATO, V. (1992) *The Teaching of Initial Literacy: How Do Teachers Do It?* London: NFER.

CLAY, M. (1993) *Reading Recovery: A Guidebook for Teachers in Training*, Auckland: Heinemann.

COX, B. (1989) *English 5–16*, London: DoE, Welsh Office.

COX, B. (1991) *Cox on Cox*, London: Routledge.

DEAN, G. (1998) *Challenging the More Able Language User*, London: David Fulton and NACE.

DfEE (1998) *The National Literacy Strategy*, London: HMSO.

DREW, D. (1987) *Caterpillar Diary*, Sydney: Thomas Nelson.

EHLERT, L. (1989) *Eating the Alphabet*, Sydney: Harcourt Brace.

GOODMAN, K. (1987) *Language and Thinking in School: A Whole School Language Curriculum*, 3rd ed., New York: Richard C. Owen.

GRAVES, D. H. (1983) *Writing: Children and Teachers at Work*, Portsmouth, NH: Heinemann.

HALL, N. (1987) *Writing With Reason*, London: Hodder and Stoughton.

HALL, N. (1996) *Learning About Punctuation*, London: Multilingual Matters.

HAYES, S. (1995) *This Is the Bear*, London: Walker Books.

HOGGART, R. (1997) 'Use of literacy', letter, *The Guardian* 24 September.

HOLDAWAY, D. (1979) *The Foundations of Literacy*, London: Ashton Scholastic.

LAYTON, L., DEENY, K. and UPTON, G. (1997) *Sound Practice: Phonological Awareness in the Classroom*, London: David Fulton.

LITERACY TASK FORCE (1997) *A Reading Revolution: How We Can Teach Every Child to Read Well*, London: RM.

LITERACY TASK FORCE (1997) *The Implementation of the National Literacy Strategy*, London: DfEE.

MEEK, M. (1988) *How Texts Teach What Readers Learn*, Stroud: Thimble Press.

MORRIS, R. (1963) *Success and Failure in Learning to Read*, Harmondsworth: Penguin.

PLANEL, C., OSBORNE, M., BROADFOOT, P. and WARD, D. (1997) *A Comparative Analysis of English and French Pupils' Attitudes to Mathematics and Language*, London: QCA.

REYNOLDS, D. (1998) 'Schooling for Literacy', *Educational Review*, **50**, 2, 30.

SLAVIN, R. E. (1996) *Success for All: A Summary of Research*. Paper presented at the annual (1996) meeting of the American Educational Research Association (San Francisco, CA, April 18–22, 1996).

TIZARD, B., BATCHFORD, P. and PLEWIS, I. (1988) *Young Children Learning in the Inner City*, Hove: Lawrence Erlbaum Associates Ltd.

VYGOTSKY, L. (1962) *Thought and Language*, Cambridge, MA: MIT Press.

WILLIAMS, E. (1997) 'A reason for rhyme', *TES*: 17 March 1997.

WOODS, D. (1988) *How Children Think and Learn*, Oxford: Basil Blackwell.

WRAY, D. (1997) *English for Primary School Teachers*, London: Letts.

Chapter 4

Grammar, spoken and written, in the National Curriculum
Bernadette Fitzgerald

> *Language is an essential part of our cultural environment, and the diffusion of coherent knowledge about language is an important aim of the English curriculum.*
> (Cox, 1989, para 5.22)

Pupils' entitlement to a grammar curriculum is outlined in the Standard Language Study section of all of the English National Curriculum programmes of study. The following is a summary of the language work which you are required to introduce at Key Stage 1 and develop at Key Stage 2:

- the importance of standard English, its grammar and vocabulary;
- the need to adapt language according to its purposes, audiences and contexts;
- antonyms and synonyms;
- the ritualised language of specific occasions such as celebrations;
- characteristic language in story telling, for instance, once upon a time;
- features of different kinds of texts: organisational, structural and presentational;
- the sentence (simple, complex, clause, phrase);
- how sentences link together within paragraphs and across texts;
- paragraphing;
- the importance of clear diction and appropriate intonation;
- the similarities and differences between the written and spoken forms of language;
- word families; and
- *use* of nouns, pronouns, verbs, adjectives, adverbs, prepositions, conjunctions, verb tenses.

Reflection

Reflection

- Were *you* taught grammar at primary school, secondary school and an HE institution?
- Did you learn about the grammar of:
    the English language, another modern language (or languages), Latin or classical Greek?
- How were you taught grammar? What effect did this have on you?
- Have you never been taught grammar? How do you feel about this?
- How would you define grammar? What does it include?
- How do you feel about teaching grammar?

> **Enquiry task 1**
>
> - Write down *your* definition of standard English. Why do you think that it is important for all pupils to be able to speak and write standard English, when appropriate? Compare your views with those contained in the articles in the Annotated Reading list at the end of this chapter. The definition in the Glossary may be helpful too.
> - How could you integrate work on standard English into a drama session with your pupils?

Grammar teaching: teachers' attitudes

The teaching of grammar in the primary school is a controversial and complex issue. All teachers, not just the language co-ordinator, will be involved in teaching grammar. Teachers bring to it their own experiences of receiving grammar teaching and attitudes towards it.

Traditionally, the model of grammar teaching which prevailed until the late 1950s was driven by a prescriptive view of language. Prescriptivism is the belief that there are set rules for the correct use of language. These rules, based on the grammar of written Latin, never varied even if and when native speakers' language differed from them (for example, prescriptively the correct form is 'It is I' although most speakers of English say 'It's me'). Another problem with this prescriptive approach is that its rules were based on correct sentence construction in formal written standard English but came to be used, inappropriately, to pass judgment on informal written language and on spoken language. This approach to grammar teaching resulted in pupils being drilled to parse, that is to label parts of speech (verbs and so on) in individual sentences. Attention was not paid to the purpose, audience, meaning or context of the writing which was being parsed.

By the early 1970s, there were significant changes in the way that English was being taught. The Bullock Report (1975) recommended an integrated approach to teaching speaking, listening, reading and writing. The emphasis was on pupils' ability to use language to communicate for real purposes and audiences in a variety of contexts. Explicit grammatical knowledge was not seen to be a prerequisite for this communication and so it declined in importance. If it was taught, it was incidentally, as an opportunity arose in the context of a pupil's own work. An alternative, descriptive approach to discussing – and teaching – language became the *modus operandi*. Descriptivism is the belief that the rules that govern how people actually use language should be systematically described. These rules are based on an analysis of samples of spoken and written language.

Recent key reports on English teaching (Cox, 1989; Kingman, 1988) have argued that there should be no return to old-fashioned, decontextualised grammar teaching:

 We have been impressed by the evidence we have received that this gives an inadequate account of the English language by treating it virtually as a branch of Latin, and constructing a rigid prescriptive code rather than a dynamic description of language in use . . .

(Kingman, 1988, para 11)

However, many teachers feel that simply to teach no grammar is not the answer either. At the end of the 1990s, the middle ground position, which was now given legislative weight by the English National Curriculum, was that:

 There are, however, more useful ways of teaching grammar than those which have been the cause of so much misunderstanding and criticism.

(Cox, 1989, para 4.24)

I would argue that only to teach grammar when it arises, by chance, in the context of a pupil's work will not result in a systematic, progressive language curriculum for all pupils. All pupils are entitled to have have an equal opportunity to experience the benefits of grammar teaching, regardless of whether a point of grammar happens, by chance, to arise in a piece of their work.

The grammar requirements of the National Curriculum have resulted in teachers adopting a more thorough and systematic approach to language teaching than was previously standard practice. Nevertheless, many teachers have expressed anxiety about being required to take a more analytical, developmental approach to grammar teaching; this anxiety was noted in the School Curriculum and Assessment Authority's Research Survey (1995). However, a structure that will scaffold teachers' delivery of a grammar curriculum is outlined in the new National Literacy Strategy's framework.

National Literacy Strategy

The National Literacy Strategy is described in some detail in Chapter 3. It offers a detailed, systematic, recursive grammar programme for pupils in the primary years. Its structure requires discrete work at word, sentence and whole text level. Principles underpinning its framework are that pupils will be able to:

- identify in real texts grammatical features which are characteristic of different genres, fiction and non-fiction;
- increasingly, talk about the effect of these grammatical features which writers have chosen to use, for instance, the use of the passive voice;
- use the grammatical understanding which they have gained as readers to inform their writing;
- learn language, learn through language and learn *about* language;
- revise and consolidate grammatical knowledge as they revisit it on this spiral language curriculum, for example a strand in the Year 6 term 3 word level work on spelling requires that pupils be taught: 'to revise and consolidate work from previous five terms . . .' (DfEE, 1998)

Metalanguage

Included in Section 3 (Appendices) of the National Literacy Strategy folder is a Technical Vocabulary list and Glossary of Terms that are used in the framework.

Whilst the glossary is introduced as 'intended for teachers', the preceding Technical Vocabulary list is described as a 'useful check list for [the] teacher. Most of these terms should also form part of the pupils' developing vocabulary for talking about language'. These terms, which are explained in the subsequent glossary, range from grapheme, onset and rime in the reception year to mnemonic, parody and tanka in Year 6. In the light of this requirement, Cox's directive is still salutary today:

 However, terms should not be introduced through drills.   (Cox, 1989, para 5.16)

Linguistic terminology is not an end itself. It is a tool to aid informed reflection on many aspects of language. This shared metalanguage adds precision to teachers' and pupils' discussions of pupils' spoken and written language. Thus, what pupils already know intuitively about language can be consolidated and extended explicitly.

 Terms are used as a way of encouraging active thinking about language and its uses.   (Cox, 1989, para 5.26)

It is worth remembering that being able to use linguistic terminology for a purpose is not the same as being able to define it out of context.

The National Literacy Strategy approach to language teaching is thus intended to be a far cry from the arid, decontextualised parsing of individual, lonely sentences which was a feature of the now discredited traditional approach to teaching prescriptive grammar. The focus now is on pupils describing language as it is used rather than as it is identified in ossified exercises. Pupils can be encouraged to act as language detectives, forming hypotheses, classifying and describing the linguistic data which they gather and forming conclusions about how language can be used.

Spoken and written language differences: a key to teaching literacy

 One of the most important topics for pupils to be able to discuss explicitly is the difference between spoken and written English. (Cox, 1989, para 5.37)

Enquiry task 2

- List two or three of the strategies and resources that you can use as a speaker that you can't use as a writer, for example, repeat a point if necessary to help a struggling listener.
- List two or three of the strategies that you can use as a writer that you can't use as a speaker, for example, leave a piece of writing and work on it again later, revising it.
- If possible, share and compare your list with a colleague.
- Compare your ideas with those in Table 4.1.
- Ask Key Stage 2 pupils to do this activity too; it will be one strategy to help them to understand, explicitly, the differences there are – and increasingly need to be – between their writing and speech.

The differences between spoken and written language are a key strand in our understanding of language variation. Spoken and written language are an integral part of everyday life for most school age children and literate adults. However, the differences between these modes of language and the consequences for children's developing literacy are often underestimated.

 An explicit awareness of the differences between speech and writing – and of the characteristic strengths and weaknesses of each mode – may provide ideas for leading pupils from the known forms and functions of speech to the unknown forms and functions of writing. (Perera, 1984)

Hopefully, teachers can now draw upon and apply the findings of linguists engaged in analysis of samples of spoken and written discourses to inform their teaching of literacy.

Children speak before they can write; they listen before they can read. The majority of children can speak one – or more – languages or dialects when they start school. The journey from speech to writing is one on which you are your pupils' guide; it is one of the most arduous and important journeys that pupils undertake. Writing is not just speech written down; speech is not a sloppy version of writing.

Spoken	Written
Both speaker and listener are present, at the same time in the same space. This allows speakers to use deictic (pointing) expressions, e.g. *It* is over *there*. What is *that*? etc: Speakers do not need to be specific in any reference to their shared surroundings.	The writer often doesn't know when her writing will be read – or by whom. Reader and writer won't share the same space, so a writer must be precise and specific, e.g. The book is on the table rather than: It is there. If the writer doesn't know who will read her work, she can't make assumptions about her readers' knowledge and attitudes.
Speakers can see their listeners' facial expressions and body language. Consequently, if a listener looks bored or puzzled, the speaker can try to make the point more clearly or succinctly.	Writers can't see the effect that their writing is having on their readers. Consequently, they have to try to predict – anticipate – any problems which the reader may experience and aim to pre-empt them.
Most spontaneous speech is transient. There is no permanent record of it. It can't be 'brought back'. When a message is verbally passed on it can be distorted.	Writing is permanent. It can be re-read and read by any one at any time.
Speech can be full of *non-sequiturs*, moving backwards and forwards over a topic, or even changing the topic under discussion. It can include repetitions and contradictions. There is no time to plan what you will say next or you could lose your turn.	It is logical and coherent with ideas connected within individual sentences and paragraphs and across a whole text. The writer can take time to look back at his work, revise and edit it.
Speech is a co-operative act: participants jointly construct the dialogue.	Writing is often a solitary act. The responsibility for constructing the text lies with the lone writer.
The speaker can use pitch, pace, tone of voice and para-linguistic features (e.g. facial expression and emphasis) to convey meaning: it's not what you say it's the way that you say it!	The writer has to learn to use a range of strategies and resources to compensate for what the voice can do, e.g. punctuation, typographic features such as use of bold, capitals or underlining to convey emphasis. She also has to supply a range of vocabulary to describe *how* words are spoken, e.g. verbs such as 'shouted, screamed'; or adverbs, e.g. . . . 'she said angrily'.
Speakers gain thinking time by hesitating and using fillers such as '. . . um, you know . . .'	Writers need to use precise vocabulary – no fillers.
The listener cannot always direct the pace of the speech. If he does not understand – or misses a point – it isn't always appropriate or possible to ask to have it repeated.	The reader can control the pace of his reading, can re-read difficult or enjoyable sections, can omit passages that do not appear to be relevant. In non-fiction texts, clues on the page (e.g. sub-headings) guide his reading.

TABLE 4.1
Differences between spoken and written language

The National Literacy Strategy's *Framework* of content for Key Stage 1 and 2 pupils includes references to characteristic features of spoken and written language – and the differences between them. It requires, for example:

Reception year **Text Level Work**
Comprehension and composition
Pupils should be taught:
Reading
Understanding of print
1 that words can be written down to be read again for a wide range of purposes
Reading Comprehension
4 to notice the difference between spoken and written forms . . . to compare 'told' versions with what the book 'says'
Writing
Understanding of print
11 to understand that writing remains constant, i.e. will always 'say' the same thing

Year 1 term 1 Reading Comprehension
3 to notice the difference between spoken and written forms through re-telling known stories; compare oral revisions with the written text

Year 3 term 1 Reading Comprehension
2 how dialogue is presented in stories

Year 5 term 1 Reading Comprehension
5 to understand dramatic conventions including: how character can be communicated in words and gesture

Year 5 term 2 Reading Comprehension
3 to explore similarities and differences between oral and written story telling

Additionally, throughout the sentence construction and punctuation strand of the *Framework*, reference is made to pupils being taught to 'understand the need for punctuation as an aid to the reader . . .' (Year 5 term 1). Teaching sentence construction and punctuation is again located in the context of the differences between spoken and written language in Year 5 term 2:

 Pupils should be taught:

- *to be aware of the differences between spoken and written language, including;*
- *conventions to guide the reader;*
- *the need for writing to make sense away from immediate context;*

■ *the use of punctuation to replace intonation, pauses, gestures;*
■ *the use of complete sentences.*   (DfEE, 1998)

Enquiry task 3

■ With differences between spoken and written language in mind, look through the fictional texts that you will be using later this term in the initial whole class, shared reading segment of the literacy hour.
■ Note instances of where authors have used strategies (e.g. punctuation, vocabulary, typography) to show how a character is feeling when he or she speaks, for example:

‘Somebody has been eating my porridge!’ said Father Bear in a great, gruff, growling voice.

‘Somebody has been eating my porridge!’ said Mother Bear in a mellow, middle-sized voice.

‘Somebody has been eating my porridge, and has eaten it all up!’ cried Baby Bear in a squeaky, little voice.

(From *The Three Bears and Goldilocks*, Langley, 1996)

■ Draw pupils' attention to these features as you help them to understand how spoken language in a fictional text operates.
■ Invite pupils to write a story, paying particular attention to strategies they use to help their readers to understand how their characters are feeling when they speak.

Case Study

A Key Stage 1 teacher who wanted to draw her pupils' attention to strategies authors used to describe how characters sounded read *Good-night, Owl* (Pat Hutchins) with them; she then spent time discussing the following extract (Figure 4.1).

Thus pupils were offered the opportunity to consolidate their knowledge, in a meaningful context, of verbs chosen to describe explicitly sounds made, and to investigate spellings of verbs which end with 'ed' (past tense). Additionally, pupils were introduced to: alliteration, assonance, onomatopoeia, commas to denote pauses, exclamation marks, the definite article and repetition used for literary effect. The teacher was delighted to find that such an enjoyable text offered so many possible avenues for exploring language. Primarily, the text had been selected as one in which pupils could take delight. Additionally, it was a resource that allowed the teacher to demonstrate how aspects of the language system worked in a real, complete text. Within the literacy hour framework, it is imperative that teachers do not see skills and knowledge about language as separate from the pursuit of meaning in a text for this is, after all, why we read.

The class went on to use *Good-night, Owl* as a model for their own creative writing: they were asked to choose a nocturnal animal as the main character and describe the sounds made by other animals which kept him awake during the daytime.

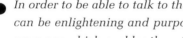

FIG 4.1
Extract from
Good-night, Owl

The bees buzzed, buzz buzz.
The squirrel cracked nuts,
crunch crunch.
The crows croaked, caw caw.
The woodpecker pecked,
rat-a-tat! rat-a-tat!
The starlings chittered,
twit-twit, twit-twit.
The jays screamed, ark ark.
The cuckoo called,
cuckoo cuckoo.
The robin peeped, pip pip.
The sparrows chirped,
cheep cheep.
The doves cooed, croo croo,
and Owl couldn't sleep.

The requirement for pupils to have an explicit working knowledge of these linguistic differences is unequivocally stated in the National Literacy Strategy's framework. This imperative is unsurprising; it can be traced back to the 1989 proposals for an English curriculum:

> *In order to be able to talk to their pupils about grammar in ways which we feel can be enlightening and purposeful, teachers will need an account of English grammar which enables them to identify and describe grammatical differences between written and spoken English . . .*
>
> (Cox, 1989, para 4.51)

Enquiry task 4

Speech and writing: different functions
- List the contexts (e.g. a doctor's prescription for medicine) in which a piece of communication needs to be written rather than spoken and the reasons why our society needs the complex process of writing.
- Ask pupils to do the same task. As they feedback their answers you can now make explicit
    - why they *need* to be able to write appropriately as well as to speak effectively
    - that the functions and structures of spoken and written forms of the language differ as do their purposes, audiences and contexts.

Responding to pupils' written language: formative assessment

> *Some of the difficulties that children experience in composing effective written language and in understanding books . . . derive from the differences between spoken and written language . . .*
>
> (Perera, 1984)

In children's own instructional or story writing, the inexperienced writer often writes just as they would have spoken it to a friend. Such writing could include:

■ colloquial, slang expressions;
■ local dialect features such as, We was late;
■ lists of often abbreviated characters' names, for example, Caz, Shar, Jase, Dar, Teen and Trace went down the road.
■ deictic (pointing) expressions, based on the misconception that the reader can read what's in the writer's mind and occupies the same physical space as the characters in the story, for example 'Put it over there,' he said. (It *may* not be obvious to the reader, who is not occupying the same time and space as the writer, what 'it' is, where 'there' is and who 'he' is.)
■ little – or no – punctuation to guide the reader as to whether someone is speaking and when they stop speaking (speech marks); no indication that a new main idea, theme or development is being introduced (paragraph indentation); no clue as to where a statement or question begins and ends (full stop, capital letter, question mark);
    – no evidence that a character is speaking with a certain emotion (exclamation mark, adverb, for example 'He said *angrily*');
    – no suggestion that the reader should pause briefly (comma).

In other words, the writer has either not understood the help her reader needs or she does not have the knowledge and skills to translate her understanding into practice.

Enquiry task 5

■ Select a piece of writing produced by one of your pupils which contains features of spoken language. Make a note of these features in the pupil's records.
■ Talk with the pupil about why these features of spoken language are inappropriate in this written work.
■ Help the pupil to suggest alternative words or punctuation marks which are appropriate to a written text.

It may help you to respond to and assess pupils' writing if the limitations outlined above are regarded and discussed as stages in pupils' journeys from speech to writing, rather than being seen simply as errors or mistakes.

The drafting process

Whilst pupils are usually willing enough to 'read through' a draft of their work, this rarely results in more than occasional corrections being made to technical errors (spellings/punctuation); most pupils proof-read their work but few tackle revising their writing – a skill required by the English National Curriculum. Pupils may be encouraged to revise their written work if you draw their attention to the needs of their absent readers who won't be able to ask for clarification if the writer has:

■ used pronouns ambiguously or

■ used a deictic expression ('we went over *there*') mistakenly assuming that the reader will know where 'there' is.

Equally, if a writer is made more aware of the need to engage her reader, she is likely to try to use a more varied vocabulary and a range of sentence constructions. Pupils need to understand that being able to revise a written text is a privilege which is enjoyed by writers as they strive to tell their readers precisely what they mean; it is a strategy which is unavailable to speakers, in most contexts, as they struggle to say just what they mean first time. Perera puts this point well:

 Learning to read and write is hard work. If young children are to see any pur-pose in their labour, it is important that they should be aware of the things that writing can do that speech cannot . . . I believe that pupils can be helped in both their reading and their writing if some of the differences between the spoken and the written modes are referred to explicitly, when appropriate, in the course of classroom activities: [these include] physical, situational, func-tional, formal, and organisational differences . . . (Perera, 1984)

Classroom contexts

To help your pupils to make explicit, extend and apply their existing implicit knowledge about the differences between spoken language and written language, you could consider adopting or adapting some of the following language activities that other teachers have used.

Case Study 1

A teacher divided her class into two large groups and asked them to form two long lines, with spaces between pupils. She gave a written message to the first pupil in one line and asked the pupils silently to pass the written message down the line. The last person to receive it, on a signal from the teacher, was asked to write the message on the board. Whilst this was happening, the teacher whispered the written message to the first pupil in the other line and instructed this group to pass the message from one to another orally, in whispers. The last pupil in this line was asked to write on the board the message he received. The teacher then invited pupils to compare the two messages on the board: both groups had been given the same message but only one of the groups was able to pass it on accurately. She considered with pupils the implications of this contrast. Why had it happened? What did it tell them about differences between written and spoken language? Why do we need the written mode?

Case Study 2

Depending on the age and reading ability of their pupils, teachers read with them one of the following stories: *Don't forget the bacon* and *The surprise party* by Pat Hutchins (Hutchins, 1993) or *Send three and fourpence we're going to a dance* by Jan Mark (Mark, 1980). They then asked pupils to consider the points which the stories make about how and why spoken language is sometimes unreliable – and its consequences. They asked them to create their own stories which included a spoken message being forgotten or distorted – with humorous consequences.

Case Study 3

A Year 6 teacher asked pupils, in pairs, to take it in turns to explain to a partner how to play a game. The partner listening was allowed to ask questions or ask for information to be repeated. The teacher taped some of these conversations and made a transcript of one of them. He then asked pupils to analyse how it differed from written rules. Finally, he asked pupils to produce a written version of the rules and contrast it with the transcript of the spoken version. On another occasion he used the same activity with the giving of directions for how to find a place. With guidance, more able pupils made a short transcript themselves.

Case Study 4

A Year 5 teacher asked pupils to consider their own daily use of spoken and written language and then produce a chart (in the form of a continuum) which shows how each *can* be formal and informal. They began by listing

- who they spoke to most and least formally and
- their most formal and informal types of writing, for example:

Speech
informal _____ *formal*
↓   ↓
best friend/pet → .... headteacher
Writing
personal diary → .... letter to a company requesting
information for a project

Implications for the teacher

Pupils sometimes experience difficulties with reading because they are encountering grammatical constructions (for example, non-finite clauses) which rarely occur in speech; thus their oral language experiences cannot scaffold their new learning. Pupils need to acquire these new forms of language in order to be competent readers, especially of non-fiction texts. There are key linguistic differences between fiction and non-fiction texts. Having mastered these differences as readers they will be able to exploit them as writers. You can help pupils by reading non-fiction (e.g. biography, travel writing) as well as stories, aloud to the class. Good non-fiction books read aloud well will offer pupils access to language and ideas which they would find too challenging to read by themselves; this will be particularly helpful to struggling readers who otherwise end up only meeting simplified language and constructions with which they are already familiar. Listening to good prose read aloud well could help pupils' development as readers and writers.

Some errors which pupils make in their writing may be recorded in their assessment portfolios and praised: they are evidence of development as pupils are experimenting with new grammatical constructions. For a detailed analysis of the linguistic difficulties experienced by pupils as they strive to write formally, see Perera (1984) in the Further Reading section.

Writing is more solitary than talking. Inexperienced writers in particular benefit from not working in isolation for long stretches of time; they will be helped – and encouraged to continue – by your responses and the feedback of their peers while the writing is being drafted. The fact that written language, unlike spoken, can be revised for real purposes and audiences makes it vital that we encourage pupils to draft, revise and edit their work.

Pupils may have a more positive attitude to drafting if they come to see it as a privilege that writers enjoy – and understand that experienced, skilled, professional, rich writers almost always do it whenever they write.

Pupils need to be aware of the differences between their spoken and written language. It is helpful for them to understand why they – and others in society – often need to write something down rather than just say it. Their writing may improve if they understand the needs of their readers. Their spontaneous spoken language will inevitably differ from their formal written language: it would sound inappropriate if this weren't the case. It would be equally inappropriate for teachers to judge pupils' spoken language as limited or careless because it is different from written language. Speech is not spoken writing!

Annotated reading list

BAIN, R. and FITZGERALD, B. and TAYLOR, M. (eds) (1992) *Looking into Language: Classroom Approaches to Knowledge about Language*, London: Hodder and Stoughton.
This book contains 36 articles which offer answers to questions such as: What can teachers do to develop pupils' knowledge about language? What classroom activities can be used to implement it? This text will be of practical interest to any teacher concerned with developing pupils' knowledge about language.

DES (1989) *English for Ages 5 to 16* (The Cox Report), London: HMSO.
This report contains a rationale for the English National Curriculum. It includes proposals about complex, controversial aspects of teaching about language. Of particular interest in the context of this chapter are: Chapter 4 (Teaching Standard English), Chapter 5 (Linguistic Terminology) and Chapter 6 (Knowledge about Language).

HARRIS, J. and WILKINSON, J. (eds) (1990) *In the Know: A Guide to English Language in the National Curriculum*, Cheltenham, Stanley Thornes.
This book provides an easy-to-read, practical introduction for teachers to issues such as Spoken and Written English (Chapter 1), Standard English (Chapter 2) and Linguistic Terminology (Chapter 11).

Further reading

BAIN, R., FITZGERALD, B. and TAYLOR, M. (eds) (1992) *Looking into Language: Classroom Approaches to Knowledge about Language*, London: Hodder and Stoughton.

CARTER, R. (ed.) (1982) *Linguistics and the Teacher*, Routledge and Kegan Paul.

CARTER, R. (ed.) (1990) *Knowledge About Language and the Curriculum: The Link Reader*, London: Hodder and Stoughton.

CRYSTAL, D. (1987) *The Cambridge Encyclopedia of Language*, Cambridge: Cambridge University Press.

DES (1989) *English for Ages 5 to 16* (Chairman, Professor Cox), London: HMSO.

DES (1975) *A Language for Life*, London: HMSO (also known as The Bullock Report).

DES (1988) *Report of the Committee of Inquiry into the Teaching of English Language* (Kingman Report), London: HMSO.

GARTON, A. and PRATT, C. (1989) *Learning to be Literate: The Development of Spoken and Written Language*, Oxford: Basil Blackwell.

HARRIS, J. and WILKINSON, J. (eds) (1990) *In the Know: A Guide to English Language in the National Curriculum*: Cheltenham; Stanley Thornes.

HUTCHINS, P. (1973) *Don't Forget the Bacon*, London: Picture Puffins.

HUTCHINS, P. (1988) *Good-night, Owl!*, London: Bodley Head.

HUTCHINS, P. (1993) *The Surprise Party*, London: Red Fox.

KRESS, G. (1982) *Learning to Write*, London: Routledge and Kegan Paul.

LANGLEY, J. (1996) *The Three Bears and Goldilocks*, London: Collins Picture Lions.

MARK, J. (1980) *'Send three and fourpence we're going to a dance'* in *Nothing to be Afraid Of*, London: Puffin.

PERERA, K. (1984) *Children's Writing and Reading, Analysing Classroom Language*, Oxford: Blackwell.

PERERA, K. (1987) *Understanding Language*, Exeter: National Association of Teachers of English (NATE).

QCA (1998) *The Grammar Papers*, London: QCA.

References

DES (1975) *A Language for Life, (The Bullock Report)*, London: HMSO.

DES (1988) *Report of Committee of Inquiry into the Teaching of English Language, (The Kingman Report)*, London: HMSO.

DES (1989) *English 5–16, (The Cox Report)*, London: HMSO.

DfEE, (1998) *National Literacy Strategy Framework for Teaching*, London: HMSO.

HUTCHINS, P. (1973) *Don't Forget the Bacon*, London: Picture Puffins.

Hutchins, P. (1988) *Good-night, Owl*, London: Bodley Head.

Hutchins, P. (1993) *The Surprise Party*, London: Red Fox.

Langley, J. (1996) *The Three Bears and Goldilocks*, London: Collins Picture Lions.

Perera, K. (1984) *Children's Writing and Reading, Analysing Classroom Language*, Oxford: Blackwell.

Chapter 5

Working with genres
John Lee

Although the idea of genre is familiar to students of literature it is probably not so familiar to English and Welsh primary teachers. It refers to how different sorts of texts may be categorised. We have not been used to thinking in this way about reading and writing up to now, but thinking about genre provides a powerful way to plan for the development of reading and writing.

Over the last 10 years or so most primary schools have adopted a process approach to the teaching of writing. They have used the ideas and suggestions from the National Writing Project to inform the teaching of writing. Principally this has meant giving children control over what they write, enabling them to write about what they are enthusiastic about, rather than setting them composition exercises. It has also stressed the nature of composition, the notion of getting children to behave like a 'real writer'. Pupils are encouraged to make successive drafts of their work and then edit it for publication. The ideas about teaching genre contained in this section assume that teachers will be familiar with the ideas of the National Writing Project, that the process of composing is normal practice.

What do we mean by genre?

A group of linguists and teachers in New South Wales, Australia, drawing on the work of Michael Halliday have produced for us some descriptions and definitions. According to these educators **genres are social processes that are constructed to fulfil particular purposes.** They are functional and each genre uses a particular vocabulary and grammar, in this way we can say they are linguistically governed. So as Peter Knapp (Cope and Kalantzis,1992) says,

❝ *Genres are the ways we get things done through language – the ways we exchange information and knowledge and interact socially.*

He then goes on to say that genres are practical and useful ways of categorising how language is used to meet our goals and needs. This view of genre takes a functional view of language. What this means for users of the language is that we make grammatical and lexical choices in order to make meaning. It is better to see grammar not as a set of rules but a system in which we can make choices.

It is important to remind ourselves here that when we speak of genres we are talking about both spoken and written texts. Genres exist in the world into which the child is born, genres pre-exist the child and it can be argued that it is the job of education to enable the child to master genres. What we are teaching children to do is make appropriate grammatical and lexical choices. A straightforward example of both points, that genres exist in the world before children, and that education seeks to teach them the mastery of them can be seen in this example of one child's work.

A letter has a clear purpose. In Figure 5.1, a pupil shows he knows what the purpose of a letter is, and has grasped the form it should take. Although

FIG 5.1
Children's writing:
a letter

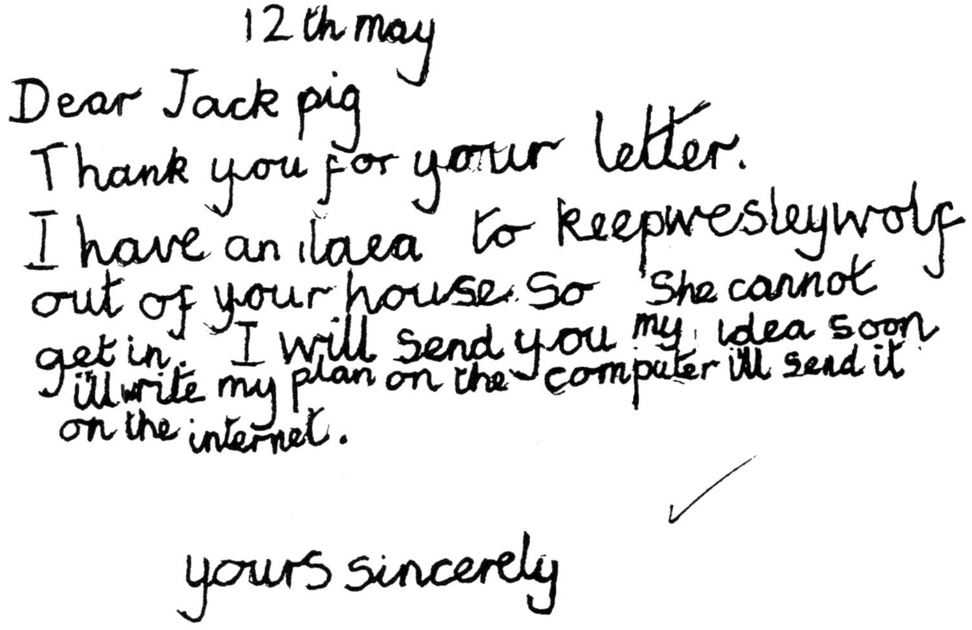

12th may
Dear Jack pig
Thank you for your letter.
I have an idea to keepwesleywolf
out of your house. So she cannot
get in. I will send you my idea soon
I'll write my plan on the computer ill send it
on the internet.

yours sincerely

FIG 5.2
Children's writing:
an argument

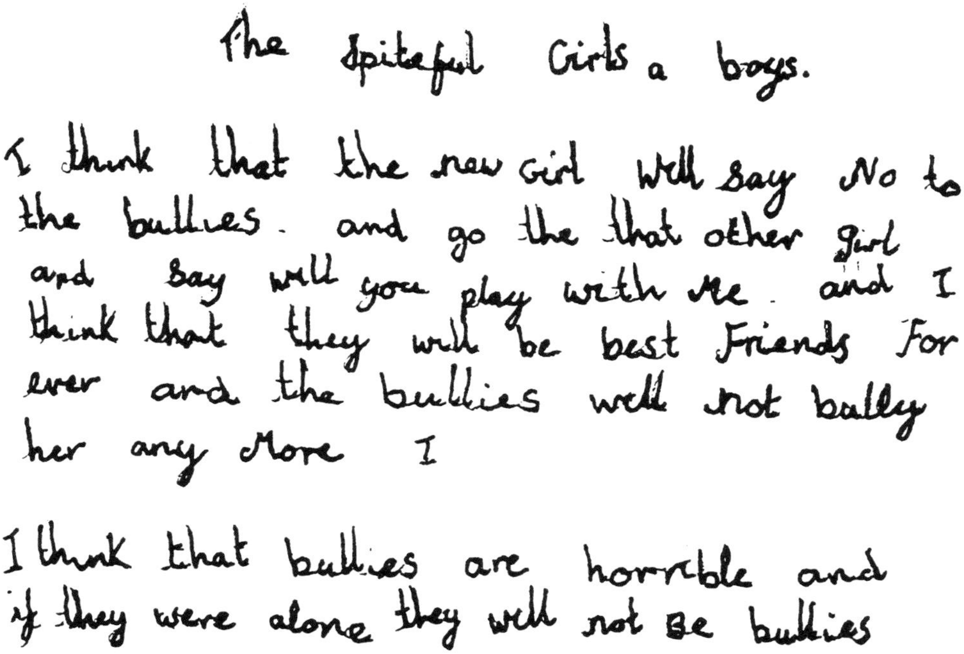

> The Spiteful Girls a boys.
>
> I think that the new Girl Well say No to the bullies. and go the that other girl and Say will you play with me. and I think that they will be best Friends For ever and the bullies well not bully her any More   I
>
> I think that bullies are horrible and if they were alone they will not Be bullies

brief, it demonstrates a developing control of the genre by this 6-year-old boy. The letter was written as a response to reading the story of the Three Little Pigs.

The conventions of most genres are not so easy to identify. If you look at Figure 5.2 you will see another 7-year-old struggling to meet the demands of the genre of argument. Asked to respond to stories and discussions about bullying this inexperienced writer simply asserts her own views.

We will return to these and other examples of children's work later in this chapter. Let us look now at a more extensive model of what genres are.

Peter Knapp one of the Australian educators referred to above has created this model of what genres are in Figure 5.3.

You will notice that this model begins with processes. What is being stressed here is the making of genres. Writers, in these cases pupils, are active language users. Let us look back to the two examples of pupils' work above. Matthew is not merely using the form of a letter, he is trying to explain what he will do in the future, but at the moment it is a secret plan. The writing in Figure 5.2 is less well worked out, being closer to speech, but even so, what we have here is an attempt to meet the demands of the process

FIG 5.3
A model for a process-based orientation to genre

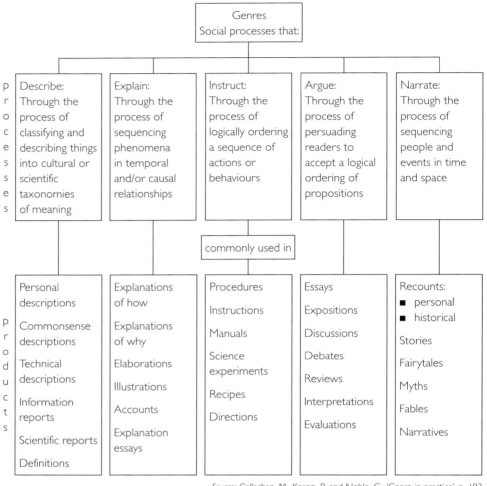

Source: Callaghan, M., Knapp, P. and Noble, G., 'Genre in practice', p. 193
in Cope, B. and Kalantzis, M. (1993) *The Powers of Literacy*, London: Falmer Press.

of argument. When we think about teaching and learning we will be very concerned with the idea of process rather than simply checking that the product meets the criteria of a particular genre.

At the same time, we must concern ourselves with what the children produce. If you look at the products specified in Knapp's model, you will see that the range of writing embodied in the National Curriculum programmes of study is represented. In addition to this we all know that we ask our pupils to read and produce 'multigeneric texts'. Our pupils are often expected to produce responses to tasks that ask them to use more than one genre. A good example of this is the class assembly where pupils may describe activities they have done, explain how and why things work and review what they have learnt up to that point. Often class assemblies use both spoken and written forms together, usually related to each other but not always so. All pupils are expected to read and interpret a wide range of genres. On a typical day Key Stage 1 pupils may listen to and read a traditional folk story, use information books to support work in science, such as classifying creatures found in a pond, and at assembly use a hymn book.

Enquiry task 1

In order to complete this task you will need access to
- class and/or school library;
- the textbooks commonly used in the class/school;
- pupils' work produced over approximately one term.

1 Take a small group of children on a 'genre walk' around the school. Get them to identify the range, variety and number of genres they see on public display.
2 Use the Knapp model and sort the texts available in the class library into the genres defined in the model.
3 How often are the pupils expected to use/consult the different genres?

Make a table like this:

Scientific	Technical explanation	Cookery books	Myth	Novels
1 per week				

Make a similar table about the children's writing.

Enquiry task 2

Review the range of occasions during which the pupils engage in speaking and listening tasks, such as circle time, show and tell, let's pretend play and presentation.

Make a table similar to the one above showing the range of genres used and the frequency of use.

Usually when we plan to teach literacy we do not confine ourselves to one form. Both inside and outside school children are exposed to a wide range of genres. They quickly come to recognise how a particular genre 'goes'. The opening 'once upon a time' will be recognised immediately as introducing a 'fairy story'. However, children do not simply recognise the form, once they become familiar with it they will 'play' with it. Children's writers often use this playfulness. The immensely popular Roald Dahl does this in his books *Revolting Rhymes* and *The BFG*, much to the delight of children and their teachers. What children also recognise is how different genres relate to each other, how some stories refer to others. This is called **intertextuality** and the best example I can think of is Alan and Janet Alhberg's book *The Jolly Postman*.

In planning to teach particular aspects of literacy many teachers accept that their pupils will be able to recognise genres, and use them as models for their own speaking and writing. Let us look at an example of this.

Case Study 1

The Three Little Pigs

Stage 1
A class of 5 and 6-year-olds use the traditional story of *The Three Little Pigs* as a theme for a unit of work. First the teacher read the children different versions of the story. They discussed the differences between the versions. While each of the versions is recognisably the 'same' story, the differences are interesting. Children considered the differences between the endings of the stories and commented on them. Data was gathered about the popularity of different versions and presented graphically.

Stage 2
The children received a letter from Jack Pig requesting help in designing a house that was 'wolf proof'.

> The Brick House
> Oink Lane
> Farmersvale
> Trottershire
> 6 May 1998
>
> Dear Mrs Shearer's class,
>
> My name is Jack Pig and you may have read about me and my brothers in *The Three Little Pigs*. I hope I don't disturb your day as your teacher will have lots of things planned for you, but I need to ask you to do something for me.
>
> Not long ago my brothers, Jeremiah and Joshua and I left home as mother pig had no room left for us in her small cottage. She did, however, warn us about Wesley Wolf, but being as excited as we were we took no notice of our mother. Jeremiah was the first to build a house. He made his house out of straw, and then Joshua made his house out of sticks. I wanted to make a much stronger house and made a brick house. Wesley Wolf soon showed up and blew both my brothers' houses down. Luckily they were able to escape and ran all the way to my house.

Now my brick house is very cramped and I fear I won't be able to keep the wolf out for long. He's already tried to trick me by getting me to go to Farmer Smith's field, Farmer Brown's apple tree, and to go with him to the fair. But so far I've managed to out-trick him. I'm scared because the wolf is now very angry. Please, please, please write to tell me how I can make my house more wolf proof, I will be eternally grateful.

Yours sincerely
Jack Pig

The format of the letter gave the children a model for their own letter writing. The children discussed the nature and purpose of the letter with the class teacher and produced a number of drafts. Matthew's letter, quoted above, was used as an example. Not all the children reached the same mastery of the genre. The important point about the discussion is that it focused on the technicalities of the genre and used children's draft texts as examples for improvement. If we look carefully at his letter (p. 170) then this becomes clearer.

Matthew's sentences are worth a careful look. His second sentence has two clauses. He uses the conjunction 'so' to introduce the dependent clause telling us that his idea will keep the wolf out of the house.

Westdean Primary School
11th May
Dear Jack Pig,
Thank you for the letter I can make a plan. This should keep Wesley Wolf out. As I know you sent a letter that said it was getting cramped. your
Sincerely Katy.

(Original spelling and layout preserved.)

In contrast Katy's text shows she has some appreciation of the form of a letter but, unlike Matthew, her letter lacks cohesion. It is a series of sentences not a piece of connected prose. Katy's letter set a challenge to the teacher. Should she be given further instruction so as to meet the genre requirements or does it represent her level of development? As in all teaching the teacher's judgement as to whether a particular child will benefit from further instruction is crucial. In this case the decision was that Katy had done very well but was not yet able to benefit from more detailed work on this genre. You may feel that further teaching would have helped her, focusing on say sentence structure and cohesion. It is worth reflecting on the fact that teachers have to make these kinds of important and difficult decisions many times each day.

In taking a genre approach to the teaching of writing it was necessary to come to a closure. This had to be more than simply finishing the work and celebrating it.

The Brick House
Oink Lane
Farmersvale
Trottershire
29 May

Dear Mrs Shearer's class,

Thank you so much for the large envelope of plans which arrived last week. You have some brilliant ideas for keeping Wesley Wolf away! We set to work at once. Joshua Pig crept out very early last Wednesday morning to put up a very high electric fence right round our garden. Jeremiah and I have been up on the roof fitting the hot water fountain. We have ordered a robot, three pairs of boxing gloves and hundreds of litres of oil from town, which should be delivered next week. My job for tomorrow is to start digging wolf traps.

We all feel so much safer now. We have been able to go out into our garden and play, and I have even started to dig my vegetable patch. I can't wait to grow my favourites – Brussels Sprouts.

Wesley Wolf does not look at all happy. He stomps around outside of the fence looking very disgruntled. He even poked his snout though a small gap yesterday but we were ready with a hammer just as you suggested. I don't think he will do that again!

Thank you once again for all your wonderful ideas, a much relieved and very happy,

Jack Pig

As you can see the teacher brought the work to a close by keeping with the genre. Jack Pig's letter reinforces the purpose and function of the genre and how it was used.

Taking a genre approach

Let's look in some detail how the teaching of writing and reading using a genre approach has been developed recently. In doing this I will make use of the work of primary school teachers from New South Wales, where this approach has been in operation for a number of years. We will begin by examining another model.

Beverly Derewianka (1990) uses this diagram to show the nature of genres.

FIG 5.4
The nature of genres

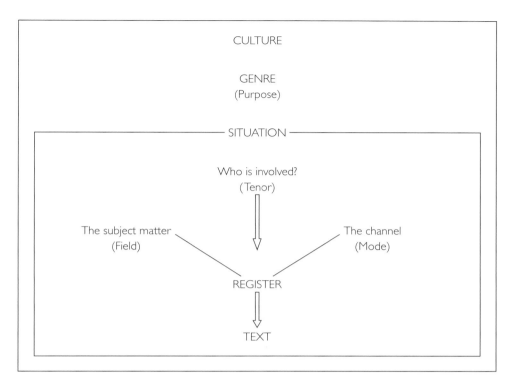

You will notice that she uses a number of technical terms drawn from linguistics. You will also have noticed that some of these terms have everyday meanings. Before looking at how the model relates to teaching English in some detail I will define some of the terms for you.

 Genres are social processes that are constructed to fulfil particular purposes. Every genre has a particular text type. Culture determines the genre of a text since cultures achieve their purposes through different language uses.

(Derewianka, 1990)

Tenor refers to the relationship between participants in a communicative act. These might be the relationship between speaker and listener or writer and reader. These relationships are often complex, for instance the relationship between a primary school teacher and the children in her class is one of unequal power but the way in which the teacher uses language will vary with her purposes.

Field is the subject matter of texts.

Mode is the medium used. It might for instance, be written, or spoken, or audio-visual, or electronic.

(Although the National Literacy Strategy ignores the new technologies it is very likely that the children we teach today will spend more time reading and writing genres using these technologies than print based media.)

Register is the way language varies in use. So the scientist who writes up her laboratory notes will not use the same genre as a reporter in a popular newspaper reporting on the scientist's experiments. Thus the register of a text is determined by its subject matter, field, its mode and the relationship of sender and receiver of a message (tenor).

Much of the advice we have been given about the teaching of writing has emphasised 'creativity', and the role of imagination. For instance Hourd and Cooper's (1959) inspirational book on children's writing makes the teacher's role that of provider of exciting experiences. More recently the work of the National Writing Project focused on independence, on the child as owner of her or his writing. The teaching of writing in primary schools is seen as one of facilitation. Children should be taught to understand the idea of audience and the process of drafting, revising and publishing but the role of the teacher as an intervener in these processes is very much in a minor key. In contrast, adopting a genre approach to the teaching of writing emphasises the teacher's role as an instructor rather than a facilitator. As you will see, to some extent the role of the teacher in teaching genre is similar to the way of teaching set out in the National Literacy Strategy.

Now let us return to Katy's letter. It clearly meets some of the kinds of things we would expect. She knows that she has to address an audience. What she has not appreciated is that the audience is unaware of what she wants to say, her message is gnomic. But what we can see is that she is able to use the 'right' register. It is a letter of the kind that 'Jack Pig' would expect. The problem is that she does not make clear what she wants to say, in terms of the model above she does not meet the demands of the field. At least with this aspect of the genre Katy has no problem with the grammatical and lexical requirements. She needs help in spelling out what her idea for a 'wolf proof' house is. But as we know Katy's teacher decided that she would not benefit for more instruction at this point.

What do genre based lessons look like?

A genre approach to teaching means that teachers must ensure that a wide range of genres is used. The National Curriculum and the National Literacy Strategy emphasise the need for us to deal with a wide range of texts. However as Gunter Kress (1994) has noted, schools tend to prioritise the reading and writing of imaginative fictional texts. He argues that schools value the kind of writing that is rarely done by people outside school.

The approach to the teaching of genre that has been most successful has begun with talk. Children of whatever age discuss texts. This discussion is guided but not directed by the teacher, it is important that children are able to comment on aspects of texts that we as teachers may not have noted.

There are some important points we need to remember when we take a genre approach to writing. I guess most of you remember being taught how to write essays at secondary school: 'First make a plan then write the essay, but make sure you put the plan at the beginning of the essay'. I wonder how many of you did what I did. First write the essay then do the plan! What I want to emphasise here is that those formulae for writing are probably not going to help children become writers. Following strict instructions means the writer does not own the writing, has no idea of audience; will not become a 'real writer'. The excellent work produced by those teachers following the National Writing Project demonstrates the importance of the understanding of audience and ownership. Trevor Cairney (1992) warns us that presenting children with models that they must follow does not lead to high quality writing. He points out that although children learn a great deal from simply reading, if they have restricted choice they will produce very formulaic writing. He contrasts the different ways that teachers can engage in talk about texts and how one approach is more productive than the other is. I have adopted many of his ideas to create the following list of recommendations.

- Remember readers and writers of texts are meaning makers.
- As often as possible let the children choose the texts.
- Use whole class interactive talk and small group independent discussion.
- Provide real purposes for the introduction of new texts.
- Use a wide variety of strategies to focus attention on texts.
- When discussing texts focus on field, tenor and register.
- Encourage the children to use correct grammatical terminology.
- Use children's own texts as well as published texts as models and examples.

You will have noticed that the work conducted using the theme of The Three Little Pigs involved consideration of different genres. First the children were engaged in reading and listening to varieties of the story, coming to an understanding of the genre of narrative. In their own writing they were concerned with letter writing, a different genre but one that was appropriate.

The children involved in this work were in Year 1. What we need to consider is how such work can be developed to meet the needs of older pupils? Here is a simple example of such work.

Case Study 2

A focus on narrative

Setting the scene
Children are reminded about the structure of narrative by asking them to recall stories they know. In particular their attention is drawn to the fact that stories have a beginning, a middle and an end, more properly an orientation, complication and resolution. The idea of a trickster story is introduced by analogy with other stories such as *Soup Stone*. Finally the children are given information about why the stories are similar, how people preserved their oral culture even though they suffered the horrors of the middle passage and slavery.

Stage 1
Read the class two related stories. The first a traditional trickster tale from Jamaica *From Tiger to Anansi* (Sherlock, 1956). The other a West African Anansi story retold by Gail Hailey (1972), *A Story, A Story*. The children are encouraged to talk about the stories, about their similarities and differences. In particular they consider the structure of narrative, orientation, complication and resolution. Both stories involve Anansi in tricking other characters and the children are asked to discuss in detail this aspect of the complication of the stories. Children are asked to discuss the following sorts of questions.

How is the story told?
What is the relationship between the author and the audience?
How does the telling of the two stories differ?
How was the complication introduced?
Did they expect it?
Could the complication be predicted from the orientation?

Stage 2
The children now read the stories in reading groups. The work is differentiated such that the able readers are challenged and the least able given adequate support. At this stage the children are asked to consider other aspects of narrative.

What sort of a character is Anansi?
Does he behave well or badly?
What motivates his actions?
Is the character of Anansi different in the two stories?
Is his motivation different in the two stories?
At this stage the children may also discuss whether the stories have a moral message or are they stories trying to explain some human action.

Stage 3
The stories provide powerful models for writing and the children are asked to write 'another one like it'. The less experienced writers are given the orientation and asked to produce the complication following the model. This work can be produced as a collaborative story.

Stage 4
Samples of the children's work are chosen and discussed with the whole class. The teacher draws attention to how well it meets the demands of the genre and asks the children to make constructive critical suggestions. The focus of this will be on the structure of the narrative so questions such as 'How is the complication introduced?' are used. The children are asked to make specific suggestions as to how the grammar of the texts can be changed to improve them. Finally the children are set the individual task of re-writing one of the texts.

The important thing to note is that both the teacher and the children make explicit comments, and where appropriate, technical terms are used.

Case Study 3

A focus on recount

A good deal of writing in school is in the form of recounts. Children are asked to say what happened. For instance after going pond dipping children may be asked to give an account of the activity and to present and marshal facts they have discovered. As with narratives recounts have a specific structure, in this case the text focuses on a sequence of events. It begins with an orientation, then offers a description of events in chronological order and finally has some sort of conclusion or general comment. Its purpose is to provide the writer with a method for reinforcing what they have learnt. It offers a way of organising experiences and is a permanent record, which can be used later.

I am going to use the example of some science work that a student of mine did with a Year 3 class. The school has an environmental study area, which has a small pond; my student planned a series of lessons on life in the pond.

The features of this simple recount are the following. On the whole the recount discussed below required children to use action verbs in the simple past tense. Such as 'dipped', 'poured', 'collected'. It required the use of technical vocabulary, in this case the names of the aquatic plants and animals. They also needed to use words such as 'next', 'first', 'then', 'afterwards' to establish the sequence of events. As this is a scientific recount on the whole personal feelings should be omitted.

General setting
The children discussed what they were likely to find in the pond. They were provided with simple recording sheets and keys to enable them to categorise and name the creatures they found. The children went in groups to the pond and dipped in order to collect the various living organisms.

Stage 1
They brought the data sheets back to the classroom and worked in groups to check that they had categorised the organisms correctly. At this point they had to decide how to present their data. In the case of this genre the use of graphical modes of recording needed to be carefully considered.

Stage 2
The children produced simple direct collaborative recounts of what they had done. These were then discussed and revised in a manner similar to that suggested for the development of narrative.

Stage 3
The ending of the written piece was discussed and a conclusion was written.

Similar plans may be made for other genres commonly demanded by school, such as these.

Genre	Examples
Instructional	How to do things. How to play a game. Recipes, manuals, directions
Reports	Topics studied, newspapers, self reporting on progress, scientific reports
Explanations	How to make a toy, how to make a circuit
Argument	Why should we be kind to animals? Can dogs think? Essays, debates, discussions

Oral work

As I said at the beginning of this chapter, genres are spoken as well as written. I want to look at some oral work and discuss how we can teach children to meet genre requirements in oral work.

One of my students was eager to engage children in the discipline of arguing. In order to do this she used a story as stimulus, to consider the problem of theft. Here is a fragment of a transcript of some children discussing a story whose theme was theft. What they are engaged in is creating an argument. This is a difficult and challenging genre for adults let alone primary school children.

1	*Teacher*:	Good. (What) do you think the author is telling the reader in this story? Some of you have mentioned it already.
2	*Paul*:	He was saying don't steal.
3	*Teacher*:	Do not steal, that's right. Mm . . .
4	*Sam*:	You'll get your just deserts in the end.
5	*Teacher*:	Do you think it's all right to steal?
6	*All*:	No.
7	*Teacher*:	No . . . why?
8	*Ann*:	'Cause it's naughty.
9	*Sam*:	It's very bad.
10	*Paul*:	It's very mean and it can upset people.
11	*Sally*:	It's um like drugs in a way cause once you steal . . . once you become addicted to it and if you keep on stealing you might get caught.
12	*Teacher*:	Yes that is what the author is saying and showing what can happen.
13	*Ann*:	If you're like a bad criminal you can get arrested.
14	*Sally*:	(referring back to the story) I don't know why it was so easy and he got away with it and nobody asks where did you get it from.
15	*Paul*:	If you steal you'll never have friends.

Lines 1–3 consist of the teacher and one of the children establishing the theme of the argument. The original stimulus for this was a story about a theft, and we see the teacher first asking about its content. In line 4 Sam adds to the theme and in doing so indicates why someone might not steal, not from a moral sense but fear of retribution. As the argument proceeds the various children begin to offer evidence and opinions. In lines 9–10, Sam and Paul build on Ann's original reason that stealing is wrong because 'it's naughty', a tautological statement. Sam echoes the statement but Paul expands and adds to it. He introduces a sense of moral order by referring to other people; he is reasoning like an ethical philosopher.

Sally then extends the argument by speculating on motivation. Why do people steal and continue to steal? Like skilled constructors of argument she uses analogy. It's like drug addiction and like drug addiction, is likely to lead to punishment, 'you might get caught'. What is perhaps noteworthy here is the use of the conditional, a very mature use of grammar. This seems to be too sophisticated for the other interlocutor who returns to the story and more simple reasoning. Paul brings the argument to a close by taking us back to line 10 where he talked about upsetting people, he now emphasises and expands it 'you'll never have friends'.

This is only a fragment of a much longer conversation, which is too long to include here. The features of the total transcript are the same. An important feature is the role of the teacher. She makes minimal interventions, prods and prompts rather than directs and lets the argument develop naturally. Many of you will already be familiar with this way of working. The National Oracy Project provided many excellent examples of such talk, and showed us all how to plan for talk as a productive learning activity.

A note about modes

Although the National Curriculum for English has clear references to modes, other than the print mode, curiously the National Literacy does not. But as I said earlier it is very likely that all of us will spend as much time reading and writing using modes different from traditional print as we will with print. This isn't all that new of course. Primary schools have made use of computer technology quite extensively over the past 20 years and both radio and television have been significant media for school use for a very long time. It is perhaps worth reminding ourselves that radio was seen as a way of providing expertise to disadvantaged rural schools in the 1930s, so arguing for the use of non-print media is not really all that radical. I want to illustrate the way in which different modes (media) are used together on a regular basis in primary schools.

The BBC programme 'Look and Read' is one of the most used educational broadcasts. It is designed for use with Year 3 and 4 pupils and its aim is the teaching of reading and, to a lesser extent, writing. The programme has accompanying booklets for the pupils and a teacher's guide. I guess that many of you use it and that even if you don't you will be familiar with it. Let's consider how it works.

The pupils watch a serial story on a week by week basis. They are encouraged to think about and discuss particular aspects of narrative, such as suspense, dramatic irony, character and motivation. When they have watched the television serial the children read the episode in print form. In addition the programme includes reading instruction. Each episode has some on-screen instructional material on reading and writing strategy. All in all the programme and its materials are a complex whole using different genre and different modes of delivery. The question is not simply how well does the programme work or how popular is it with children but how these different genres and modes of presentation relate to each other.

> **Enquiry task 3**
>
> In order to complete this task you will need access to the BBC programme 'Look and Read' and its accompanying materials.
> 1 How closely does the printed text replicate the television story?
> 2 In what ways do you think the narrative is different when read rather than viewed? You might like to consider the idea of immediacy against the way that print allows or encourages re-reading and revision.
> 3 Look at the instructional material in one episode and compare it with the printed materials and the suggestions that are given to teachers in the teacher's booklet. Is one more effective than the other?

There has been a great debate about whether the mode we use changes what we are learning and how we learn it. In the case of using a genre approach we can give this detailed consideration because it becomes very obvious that there are some things we can do in print that can't be done on film or television. The reverse is also true. Finally, when we come to consider computer technology the control over the ebb and flow of information that many computer programmes give may constitute new and exciting genres. Even the early and now quite primitive adventure games give children a control over the complication of narrative that is not so easily available in printed texts.

Conclusion

In this chapter I have focused on the idea of teaching genre. I have not attempted to cover all aspects of the National Curriculum for English, there are already many books that do that. I have argued that genres are social processes and that by thinking about genres we can construe children as active language users. It is this focus on the idea that language users have a clear purpose in mind, know their audience and choose language functions accordingly.

I made a very brief comment on the important topic of mode/media and also indicated how a genre approach is closely related to the work of the National Writing Project and the Oracy Project. Its ideas are also very compatible with the National Literacy Strategy.

Annotated reading list

There is a developing body of literature on the teaching of genre. I have chosen the following two as most accessible and useful. If you want to read in greater depth both of these books have good up-to-date bibliographies, and journals such as *Primary English* and *Reading* have short articles that are relevant.

KRESS, G. (1994) *Learning to Write* (2nd edition), London: Routledge.
Gunter Kress offers a comprehensive account of the teaching of writing to primary school children using an approach drawn from functional linguistics and genre theory. It has some excellent practical examples and analysis of children's writing but does not shy away from theory.

DEREWIANKA, B. (1990) *Exploring How Texts Work*, Newtown NSW, Australia: Primary English Teaching Association.
This book was written to introduce primary school teachers to some of the ideas of using genre approaches to the teaching of reading and writing. It has some excellent practical examples, and is clear and accessible.

References

CAIRNEY, T. (1992) 'Mountain or molehill: the genre debate viewed from "Down Under"', *Reading*, April, pp. 23–9.

COPE, B. and KALANTZIS, M. (1993) *The Power of Literacy: A Genre Approach to Teaching Writing*, London: Falmer Press.

DEREWIANKA, B. (1990) *Exploring How Texts Work*, Newtown NSW: Primary English Teaching Association.

FRANKLIN, S. (1994) 'Finding the right words', *Special Children*, February 1994, pp. 13–14.

FRANKLIN, S. (1998) 'Writing, the novel and genres – an English perspective', *English in Education*, **32**, 2, pp. 25–34.

HAILEY, G. (1972) *A Story A Story*, London: Macmillan.

HALLIDAY, M. A. K. (1993) 'Towards a language-based theory of learning', *Linguistics and Education*, **5**, 2, pp. 93–116.

HOURD, M. L. and COOPER, G. E. (1959) *Coming Into Their Own*, London: Heinemann.

KRESS, G. (1994) *Learning to Write* (2nd edition), London: Routledge.

SHERLOCK, P. (1956) *Anansi the Spiderman: Jamaican Folk Tales*, London: Macmillan.

Chapter 6

Mathematics: aims and practices
Ruth Sharpe

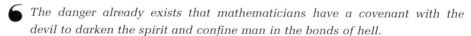
The danger already exists that mathematicians have a covenant with the devil to darken the spirit and confine man in the bonds of hell.

(St Augustine, C400 AD)

Introduction

It is not unusual to hear adults express negative attitudes towards mathematics. At a parents' evening on mathematics education I asked the audience to share their thoughts on the subject and the most common responses reflected feelings of dislike and even hatred. 'It was frightening, daunting'. 'It made you panic', they said. Parents recalled classroom experiences where they had felt humiliated and confused. None said they enjoyed it or that it was in any way pleasurable. Nevertheless, there were none who said that mathematics should not be taught. The second most common response, in fact, was that it was very useful. It explained the way things worked, it helped you do your shopping, it was a means of solving problems. One parent worked in a technical job and explained that he used mathematics in his work but even so added, 'not the kind you are taught at school'. The third most popular response was that mathematics was important because it was a way of thinking. It was a discipline for study, a kind of logical thinking, a means of exercising the brain and showing you were clever.

The view that mathematics is an essential component of statutory schooling is one that most people would share. It can be said that with or without the National Curriculum mathematics has held a central place in the primary curriculum since the introduction of statutory education in 1870. Most would accept the high status accorded to mathematics in children's education and most would accept that it should be both useful and intellectually challenging. However, not all would agree on the kinds of activities to be offered to children that would meet these aims and there is probably even less agreement on how they should be achieved.

Mathematics: practical skill or mental discipline?

The belief that mathematics should be useful is predicated on a view of mathematics as a tool for solving real life problems. This view holds that the content of the curriculum should serve the needs of society and teach the skills and knowledge that will enable individuals both to contribute to the economic development of the community and deal effectively with the mathematical demands of everyday life. The emphasis here is on utilitarian applications of mathematical knowledge with the aim of enabling individuals to function in and contribute to the society in which they live.

On the other hand, the view that mathematics is an intellectual activity is to do with abstract concepts of human mental endeavour and achievement. The content of the curriculum in this context should enable the individual to develop an aesthetic and intellectual appreciation of what Griffiths and Howson (1974) described as 'controlled imaginative thought' (p. 7). Learning mathematics should enable individuals to enjoy the analysis and study of mathematical relationships and numerical and geometric structures and create and develop new mathematical ideas. The emphasis here is on abstract logical thought and although this inevitably becomes the foundation for discoveries that have practical applications, the main purpose is the study of mathematics for its own sake.

Each of these views of the curriculum can be recognised in the responses of parents mentioned at the beginning of this chapter. Although both views reflect different perspectives about the nature and purpose of mathematical knowledge and understanding they are not incompatible and may coexist and even support and complement each other. Thus, as Griffiths and Howson (1974) suggest, the Egyptians used mathematics to help them with complex building programmes and to control the environment, whilst their priests were revered for their 'mystical' ability to understand theoretical problems of mathematical logic. Similarly, the identification of Pure and Applied mathematics as separate aspects of GCE A level syllabi may be seen as an acknowledgment of the dual components of the curriculum – a view also shared by the authors of the *Non-statutory Guidance for Mathematics* (1989) who stated that:

 Mathematics is not only taught because it is useful. It should also be a source of delight and wonder, offering pupils intellectual excitement and an appreciation of its essential creativity.

(NCC, 1989, p. A3)

In tracing the history of mathematics curricula since the beginning of statutory education both elements of mathematics are evident, although it could be argued that utilitarian mathematics is traditionally the province of the primary school whilst the more abstract areas of mathematical thought (for example, theorems and proofs) have tended to be located in secondary school syllabi.

The emphasis on arithmetic and computation that formed the bedrock of elementary school children's experiences in the early part of the twentieth century reflected the perceived usefulness of these computational skills in the world of work. (See, for example, Howson, 1982). In the early 1950s, as the mathematical demands of society became more complex, a broader vision of mathematics emerged with the publication of the Mathematical Association's report *The Teaching of Mathematics in the Primary School* (Mathematical Association, 1955). The report argued that arithmetic in primary schools was only a component of the wider subject of mathematics and that it should be viewed not as an end in itself, but as a means of access to the broader areas. Thus, the two elements of mathematics were seen as supporting and complementing each other:

 The science of number is a part of our culture and an ability to understand and use number is a fundamental social need. . . . Arithmetic leads on to algebra . . . and the subject develops through algebra and trigonometry to calculus and co-ordinate geometry.

(p. 2)

The report discussed the 'new' topics of binary scales, sets, groups, matrices, statistics and probability and heralded the emergence of the so-called Modern Mathematics movement. Indicative of the developments in primary schools at the time was the establishment in 1964 of the Nuffield Foundation Primary Mathematics Project.

The declared objective of the project was to produce a course of mathematics for children from 5 to 13 (see Schools Council, 1965, pp. 102–103). The results of the project's work may be seen in *Nuffield Maths*, a scheme of work for 5–11 year-olds, that remains (although revised) popular today. The

Nuffield Mathematics Scheme provided the blueprint for subsequent commercial mathematics schemes and provided eloquent testimony to the expanding vision of the mathematics content at primary level. It included a wide range of 'real life' measurement activities (as opposed to pseudo real measurement designed to develop computation skills) and references to shape and space. The Nuffield Project also drew heavily on the work of Piaget[1] (see for example Mogford, 1966, pp. 1–5; Griffiths and Howson, 1974, pp. 79–82; Ernest 1991, p. 102 and p. 189) and in so doing reflected the prevailing orthodoxy of the mathematics educational community. Two aspects of Piaget's theories are of particular relevance. Ernest (1991) describes the first of these as a hierarchical view of mathematics learning (p. 238). This theory postulates that there is a sequence of four stages of learning which form a hierarchy of development and that each stage must be mastered before the learner is ready to 'think and operate at the next level' (ibid.). The second is the concept of conservation that Piaget (1941) applied to mathematics. He wrote that:

> *Conservation is a necessary condition for all rational activity . . . A set or collection is only conceivable if it remains unchanged irrespective of the changes occurring in the relationship between the elements . . . whether it be a matter of the child's earliest contacts with number or of the most refined axiomatizations of any intuitive system, in each and every case the conservation of something is postulated as a necessary condition for any mathematical understanding.* (pp. 3–4)

Williams and Shuard (1994) epitomised this approach to mathematics in their seminal work *Primary Mathematics Today*. This text has since been revised and up-dated but is still underwritten by the Piagetian model of stages of development and the appropriate teaching to develop the theories of sets, relations and equivalence that underpins the mathematics of conservation.

Further modifications were made to the concept of a primary mathematics curriculum in 1982 with the publication of *Mathematics Counts*, the report of a committee of enquiry into the teaching of mathematics in schools (often referred to as the *Cockcroft Report*, Cockcroft, 1982). The terms of reference for the report required the committee to consider the teaching of mathematics 'with particular regard to the mathematics required in further and higher education, employment and adult life' (Cockcroft, 1982, p. iii). In defining the primary curriculum Cockcroft argued that mathematics should 'enrich children's aesthetic and linguistic experiences' (para. 287) as well as developing powers of logic and reasoning and 'equipping them with the

numerical skills which will be a powerful tool for later work and study'
(ibid.).

Ernest (1991) suggests that the emphasis throughout the report is 'clearly
utilitarian' and describes the envisaged curriculum as representing
'technological pragmatist aims' (p. 221). He supports this view by citing
Cockcroft's 'Foundation List' of basic mathematical skills which Ernest
describes as serving the goals of industrial trainers.

The curriculum of the Cockcroft report was, however, an advisory one:
although there was considerable funding to support teacher development
there was no legal requirement for teachers to adopt the committee's
recommendations. The 1988 Education Reform Act introduced, for the first
time, a minimum mathematics curriculum backed by statute. Although there
have been two revisions to the National Curriculum for mathematics, the
content topics remained essentially those identified in the Cockcroft report:
that is number and algebra, data handling, shape, space and measure.
The uses and applications of mathematics, whilst included as distinct
programmes of study, reflect the purposes of mathematical study and the
methods and strategies to be employed rather than a separate topic to be
learnt. It does however suggest that mathematics should be taught both
because it is useful and because it is an area of intellectual endeavour of
value in its own right. This is eloquently illustrated by the first programme
of study for using and applying mathematics at all four key stages which
states that pupils should be given opportunities to:

*Use and apply mathematics in practical tasks, in real life problems and within
mathematics itself.*

The non-statutory guidance states unequivocally that:

*Mathematics provides a way of viewing and making sense of the world. It is
used to analyse and communicate information and ideas and to tackle a wide
range of practical tasks and real-life problems.*

*Mathematics also provides the materials and means for creating new imagin-
ative worlds to explore. Through exploration within mathematics itself, new
mathematics is created and current ideas are modified and extended.*

(NCC, 1989, p. A2)

The comprehensive and inclusive nature of the National Curriculum
requirements has not, however, received universal endorsement. Despite the

two re-writes of the curriculum the apparent failure of pupils in the United Kingdom (UK) to perform in mathematics against international comparisons regenerated concerns about both the content of the mathematics curriculum and the way that mathematics is taught. Reynolds and Farrell (1996) identified these concerns in their review of International Surveys of Educational Achievement (entitled *Worlds Apart?*). The focus for the study was on science as well as mathematics partly because:

 Mathematics and Science are universally recognised as the key skills needed in a modern industrial society, and particularly in new 'information age' economies. (p. 1)

Although this report highlighted pedagogical issues rather than curriculum ones the identification of mathematics as a key skill implies a view of its utilitarian nature. It would seem to suggest that a main aim for teaching mathematics is to enable pupils to support the needs of an advanced technological society. It is not my intention here to present a critique of the international research studies investigated for the report but you may wish to speculate how far these studies assessed the kind of mathematics that would enable pupils to develop the skills needed to contribute to 'information age' technologies.

However, the report renewed interest in the teaching of mathematics and in particular the debate about 'falling standards'. In 1996 the National Numeracy Project was set up with the aim of improving standards as a result of 'an accumulation of inspection, research and test evidence [which] has pointed to a need to improve standards of numeracy' (National Numeracy Project, 1998, p. 4). The *Framework* document has not attempted to redefine the content of the mathematics curriculum nor has it sought to clarify the aims of mathematics teaching. It has sought instead 'to illustrate how the programmes of study can be planned and taught in each year' (ibid., p. 7) and it has maintained that the *Framework* 'covers all aspects of the National Curriculum for mathematics'.

In summary, the curriculum for mathematics in this country has been consistently framed with a view to both teaching the utilitarian and practical aspects of mathematics as well as the intellectual and abstract. There has perhaps been more emphasis on the former, particularly in the primary school. Where utilitarian purposes have been evident they have, at least in intent, sought to respond to the developing economic needs of the workplace, the demands of further and higher education and the increasingly complex mathematical needs of individuals in everyday life.

Enquiry task 1

1 Keep a diary over a week.
  Note down everything you do in your daily and working life that involves the use of mathematics.
  Include examples of:
      logic and reasoning;
      the use of measures;
      any calculations you do (and how you do them);
      any time when you make use of knowledge and understanding in shape and space;
      any occasions when you are using, manipulating or interpreting statistical information.
2 Reflect on how you know how to do these things, how you have learnt them. Particularly consider
  your school experiences and identify what was taught to you in the classroom and at what age you
  learnt to do various things.
3 Compare your findings and conclusions with the National Curriculum programmes of study.
4 Look at your school's policy document for mathematics. Consider how far the aims and objectives
  reflect both the applications of mathematics and mathematics as an intellectual activity.

Mathematics: teaching and learning

The teaching of mathematics has had a more controversial history, perhaps, than the nature of the material to be taught. The media and some politicians appear to centre the debate around two kinds of teaching often simplistically described as 'traditional' and 'progressive'. The former has become associated with a 'back-to-basics' view of teaching and the latter, invariably used in a pejorative sense, associated variously with post-Plowden primary schools, discovery methods and 'trendy' ideas. Such extreme views are unhelpful. They owe little to either the work of serious theorists and researchers or to actual practice in school. This does not mean to say that there are not different styles of teaching or different beliefs about what constitutes good practice. The past century has witnessed a range of alternative theories and practices. One of the most useful classifications of practices and beliefs about practice can be found in a study undertaken by Askew, Brown, Rhodes, Johnson and William (1997) on behalf of the Teacher Training Agency. The study identified three different 'teacher orientations' related to the beliefs of primary practitioners in relation to the teaching of number (pp. 24–46). Although this research was based on Case Studies of contemporary teachers, the orientations are by no means new and there are strands within them that can be recognised as describing teaching approaches that have been advocated by theorists or practised by teachers in the past.

Perhaps the most easily identified of these is the *Transmission Orientation*. In this model teachers characteristically believe that success is measured by the ability to perform standard procedures correctly. Teaching is instruction based and is seen as separate from and having priority over learning. There is a reliance on verbal explanations, the learning of rules and 'pencil and paper' drill and practise. The mathematics curriculum is viewed as having discrete elements and pupils learn standard algorithms for performing calculations, learn techniques and routines and commit such routines to memory. This approach is not an unfamiliar one and many adults today may recognise this as the way they themselves were taught mathematics. The emphasis here is on rote learning, the acquisition of facts and skills and the compartmentalisation of mathematical ideas into discrete packages.

Askew's *Discovery Orientation*, on the other hand, is more closely linked to the Piagetian model associated with developments in primary mathematics in the 1960s and 1970s. Teachers using this approach are described as believing that learning is separate from and has priority over teaching. Learning is achieved through practical experience and exploration with the use of a variety of practical resources. Progress is individualised and linked to the concepts of readiness and stages of development. Pupils engage in individual activities linked to their stage of development and much emphasis is placed on the use of practical apparatus to model new concepts being learnt. This has echoes of Piagetian theories, discussed above, which suggested that there is a sequence of four stages of learning which form a hierarchy of development and that each stage must be mastered before the learner is ready to think and operate at the next level. The emphasis is on children developing their own methods as and when they are ready to do so but being provided with practical materials to establish models for the abstract ideas to be learnt at the next stage of development.

The third orientation is associated with the *Connectionist* teacher. In this model the teacher believes that learning is achieved through 'purposeful interpersonal activity based on interactions with others' (p. 31) and that pupils learn through 'being challenged and struggling to overcome difficulties' (ibid.). The main characteristic of the connectionist teacher would appear to be an awareness of links between different aspects of mathematics and an ability to make these connections explicit in their work with children. Pupils develop personal strategies for calculation, which are refined by the teacher, and errors and misconceptions are recognised and worked on. The 'interpersonal' aspect of the Connectionist model is not unlike the social constructivist approach with children being supported in moving from an existing state of knowing and understanding to the next stage of development through their interactions with more experienced others – adults and other children.

It could be argued that the kind of teaching described as connectionist in Askew's work is consistent with the teaching and learning styles advocated by the Cockcroft committee in 1982. Cockcroft argued that exposition by the teacher and discussion between pupil and teacher and pupils themselves should form the basis of good teaching together with practice, practical work, problem solving and investigation (paragraph 243). The National Curriculum for mathematics, whilst not attempting to define pedagogy, places a clear emphasis on questioning and discussion, the inter-relationship of different aspects of the curriculum and the importance of purposeful and meaningful activities. Askew's report argued that connectionist orientation is the most consistently successful in the teaching of numeracy.

Enquiry task 2

1 Consider your experiences as a learner of mathematics and compare them with the three models described above. Which model best describes the way in which you were taught mathematics?
2 Critically examine your own beliefs about your teaching and pupils' learning of mathematics. Which model best describes your personal perspective?

Aims and practices in school

It has been suggested above that mathematics is taught both because it is useful and because it is an area of intellectual endeavour. It was also suggested that the definition of what is useful in mathematics changes with the developing and changing needs of societies and individuals. However, the intended aims for teaching mathematics, no matter how worthy these may be, are not necessarily those that are achieved. To say that what we intend pupils to learn, whether this be useful or intellectually stimulating, does not necessarily reflect what is actually happening in schools. Similarly theories about teaching and learning, no matter how well founded, may not accurately reflect real practice. The 'orientations' described above are drawn from research investigating the attitudes and beliefs of contemporary teachers, but these teachers are not typical. Schools were identified by the research project on the basis of 'being already known to be performing well above expectation in relation to numeracy' (p. 9). It cannot be said, therefore, that the models are in any sense representative (or intended to be representative) of primary teachers in the UK. To illustrate the potential for mismatch between theory and practice in the school setting, two Case Studies are presented below.

Case Study 1

Aims for teaching mathematics and classroom practice

The school is in the affluent suburbs of a large town. It has a clear and coherent mathematics policy that has been devised by the staff working together under the management of an enthusiastic mathematics co-ordinator. The aims for teaching mathematics have been agreed and endorsed by all members of staff. They include the following:

To develop in children
- a positive attitude towards mathematics as an interesting and valuable subject;
- an ability to think clearly and logically in mathematics with confidence, independence of thought and flexibility of mind;
- an appreciation of mathematical structures, patterns and the ability to identify relationships;
- an awareness of the uses of mathematics in the world beyond the classroom. Children should be aware that mathematics will frequently help them to solve problems they meet in everyday life or understand better many of the things they see, and provide opportunities for them to satisfy their curiosity and to use their creative abilities;
- an awareness of problem solving strategies.

Kelly is 9 years old and is in a Year 3 junior class in the school. The class is 'ability grouped' for mathematics, that is the children sit at tables according to the level of their maths book in a published scheme. There are three boys on the 'top' table, which is positioned next to where Kelly sits on the 'bottom' table. She sits on her own as no other children in the class are on the same book. She appears to be aware of her status as the 'top' boys are inclined to taunt her for doing 'easy' work. The teacher makes every effort to stop them doing this and to reassure Kelly that there are probably things she can do that the boys cannot, although she is not clear what these things are.

Kelly works very slowly on her maths work (which is taken entirely from the scheme book) and makes every effort to produce careful neat work. She is rarely successful in getting the right answer and doesn't seem to know what is required of her. She constantly asks for the teacher's attention when doing her maths, but despite repeated explanations from the teacher she still manages to get it wrong.

She is very slow in getting any work done 'on paper', is often in tears and despite being kept in at playtime or given work to take home to 'catch up', she is falling further and further behind the other children in the class. The teacher has suggested that her parents are not very supportive at home and often don't seem to know themselves what is required of a piece of work.

Kelly is also a poor reader in that she is on the lowest reading scheme book in her classroom and finds it difficult to read the instructions in her maths book. The teacher feels that it would be detrimental to Kelly to allow the other children to help her as she would never learn to 'stand on her own feet' and besides, it would disrupt their work. On one occasion Kelly was working on a page with pictures of a number of objects and two arrows with 'is lighter than' and 'is heavier than' written next to them. The instruction said that a balance would be needed but did not say why. The task for Kelly was to draw the correct arrows between pairs of pictures. After some minutes Kelly joined the queue at her teacher's desk. The teacher asked if Kelly knew what 'heavier than' meant and Kelly nodded uncertainly. The teacher then asked if she knew what 'lighter than' meant and again she responded with a hesitant nod. The teacher then explained that all she had to do was put the right arrows between the right pictures. Kelly went away. By break-time she had drawn a few arrows between pictures. Some arrows had been drawn and rubbed out. None seemed to relate to the instructions for the task.

I would argue that weighing is a useful practical skill that children should acquire and that this activity is, in intention, perfectly consistent with the aim of developing that skill. However, it is clearly not helping Kelly to learn that mathematics will help her to 'solve problems in everyday life' as it bears no relationship to real life weighing or the practical circumstance in which such skills are used. Kelly, in fact, may be learning instead that mathematics is a fairly pointless activity that serves no useful purpose at all. There are of course other issues here to do with Kelly's personal qualities. It may be that she has already learnt to dislike mathematics and that the seeds have been sown for the negative attitudes expressed by the parents in the introduction to this chapter.

Enquiry task 3

1 Compare the aims for teaching mathematics in Kelly's school with the account of Kelly's classroom experiences.
2 Imagine you are Kelly's teacher.
   ■ Analyse Kelly's difficulties and think how you would deal with them.
   ■ Devise an activity that would enable her to develop real weighing skills.
   ■ Devise an activity that will enable her to develop intellectual curiosity through investigating the properties of solid shapes.

Case Study 2

Classroom practice and children's learning

Lisa is just 6. She is a child of 'average' ability and has not displayed any difficulties in completing mathematics tasks set her. She has mastered one-to-one correspondence, has made sets of numbers up to 10, can count accurately to at least 20 and has learnt to do addition by combining sets of numbers. She is beginning to learn about subtraction and is using a commercial scheme, which introduces subtraction as the difference between sets. Her current work consists of identifying differences through matching and colouring. That is, she has been given a work card with sets of different numbers of circles with a sum underneath with the requirement to 'match and colour the difference'. For example:

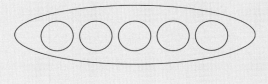

$$5 - 3 = \boxed{}$$

In the case of the example above, she is required to match by putting crosses on three of the circles, colour in the remaining two and write a '2' in the empty box. She has eight problems of this kind to solve. To make the task easier and to reduce errors in copying, she has been asked to trace the work card. This is what Lisa did:

1　She began by writing the answers to all eight sums.
2　Next, she copied over all the 'sums', carefully tracing the little boxes around the answers she had already written.
3　She traced the oval set-rings.
4　She started tracing all the little circles.

Lisa in fact did not do what she was supposed to do but worked the problem backwards starting with the answer and then trying to work out how it should have been achieved. In asking her what she thought she was doing Lisa's response was frank. 'I dunno,' she said, and then, pointing at the circles, 'but I've got to do all they bleedin' little eggs.'

A number of issues become apparent from this observation. The first is that Lisa already knows the answers to simple subtraction sums of this kind. The second is that the carefully prescribed progression has very little to do with Lisa's *actual* intellectual development. It is a view of progression that is drawn from a careful analysis of the mathematics involved made by someone who already understands it. It in fact bears no relationship to the way Lisa thinks about the numbers nor is it helping her to solve problems of this kind. Thirdly, not only is Lisa effectively wasting her time she is also learning that there are some things you do in mathematics that make no kind of sense, but that you have to do them anyway. It may only be a matter of time before the requirement to solve problems like this through an apparent 'approved' method will take precedence over her own common-sense understanding of how the numbers work. The Cockcroft Report argued that such attitudes to mathematics could incur feelings of guilt and cites adults who, when asked to perform calculations, 'felt a sense of inadequacy because they were aware that they did not use what they considered to be the "proper" method' (paragraph 22).

Enquiry task 4

1 Mentally work out the answer to the following sum:

$$18 \times 6$$

2 Try to write down the stages you went through to get the answer. For example you might decide it is easier to multiply 6 by 20 and take away two 6s. Your stages could look something like this:
   18 to 20 adds on 2
   6×20 is the same as $6 \times 2 \times 10$ or $12 \times 10 = 120$
   $2 \times 6 = 12$
   12 is $10 + 2$
   $120 - 10 = 110$
   $110 - 2 = 108$
3 Decide which stages are 'instant recall' and which need an understanding of the relationships in number.
4 Compare your method to the way you were taught multiplication at school.
5 Compare your method with the way you teach children to do calculations.
6 Ask friends, colleagues to do the same sum in their heads – collect as many different ways as you can for doing this sum.

I would suggest that in both the Case Studies described above the children are neither learning about the usefulness of mathematics, nor the intellectual challenge that it can offer. The mathematics they are doing is not really much at all beyond obeying instructions. Worse, both children may be learning that mathematics is not only a purposeless activity but that it is disagreeable and mystifying. These two examples may not be typical of what children are doing in primary schools. However, you may wish to think about the evidence that suggests that the majority of children work from commercially produced schemes, working in isolation through procedural exercises and pre-programmed learning. It is my belief that the structure and content of commercial schemes invite the kind of experiences enjoyed by both Kelly and Lisa. The following extracts taken from HMI reports offer a view of pupils' experiences, which can be recognised as comparable with the experiences of these two girls:

> *Ninety-nine per cent of schools use commercial schemes, most on an individualised basis.* (DES, 1994)

There was often undue pressure on the pupils to record mathematics formally before their understanding had been adequately developed. (Ibid.)

What is taught [in mathematics] and its pace and differentiation is still overtly determined by an undue reliance on published schemes, rather than on a sound appreciation of what children are capable of doing given good teaching. (DES, 1993)

Much of the mathematics seen involved individualised working . . . even when pupils were said to be working in groups or as a class, they were often in reality working individually. (DES, 1991)

. . . there was undue reliance on [mathematics schemes] in most schools. The consequences included a lack of differentiation, mathematics learning based on texts with pupils simply carrying out step by step instructions rather than on 'contexts', restricted mathematical thinking, and poorly developed understanding. (DES, 1992)

You may wish to consider how commercial mathematics schemes prescribe not only what is taught but also the approach to be used and the management and organisational strategies to be employed. Such materials, whilst addressing the content of the National Curriculum, seem to have a tendency to present mathematics in a particular ordered sequence and focus on the acquisition of facts and skills. I would suggest that they compartmentalise mathematics into discrete elements and, as evidenced by the individual work books, work cards and text books, are aimed at the individual working alone through a pre-sequenced order of progression. In describing the orientation of the scheme, I would suggest that it appears to be a cross between the discovery approach (linked to a linear sequence of 'readiness' and the use of practical activities to precede the written work) and the transmission approach with a focus on the acquisition of discrete facts, skills and routines. You may wish to think about how a scheme could be written in a way that would enable children and teachers to focus on the processes of mathematical thinking and creative problem solving. I believe that these processes are beyond the scope of these schemes as they are to do with ways in which children perform as mathematicians. To teach these processes demands flexibility and invention in a progression of learning that cannot be predicted.

My own research (Sharpe, 1998) suggests that despite criticisms of scheme use, they continue to be the dominant influence on children's mathematical experiences. My research also suggests that the 'step by step' approach to learning, common to most schemes, reflects the way teachers themselves were taught mathematics and hence has the appeal of a recognised orthodoxy. In a study of mathematics co-ordinators attending 20 day GEST funded courses (Sharpe, 1995) I found that:

The notion of thinking mathematically, experimenting, hypothesising, pattern finding and reasoning had been, for the vast majority, an unfamiliar experience.

(p. 7)

One teacher I interviewed told me she taught rules and procedures because she had no experience of any other approach to teaching mathematics and that the linear progression of the commercially produced scheme she used was 'common sense'.

It would seem that most teachers have experienced mathematics predominantly as a content-based subject essentially learnt to achieve examination success. The typical examination syllabus does not require pupils to use and apply their knowledge, skills and understanding, nor does it foster independent creative mathematical thought. The structure of the commercial scheme would seem to support this view of mathematics with its emphasis on knowledge and facts to be learnt and skills and techniques to be acquired. This may not be surprising, given that scheme authors are also likely to have experienced this kind of mathematics at school and, judging by the claims of publishers, been rather good at it. Ahmed (1987) suggested that for most people their thinking about the nature of mathematics was modelled on their school experiences and that

Mathematics seems to be understood by most people to be a body of estab-lished knowledge and procedures – facts and rules . . . However, most math-ematicians would see this as a narrow view of their subject. It denies the value of mathematics as an activity in which to engage. Decision making, experi-menting, hypothesising, generalising, modelling, communicating, interpreting, proving, symbolising and pattern finding are all integral parts of that activity. Without engaging in processes such as these, no mathematician would have been able to create the procedures and systems mentioned above in the first place.

(p. 13)

Reflection

Think about how you learned mathematics at school and try to recall if you ever engaged in the activities described by Ahmed as 'real' mathematics.

My research suggests that teachers' experiences of learning mathematics sustain an acceptance of scheme use and a justification for it. They make alternative approaches difficult to defend in personal practice and to colleagues and parents. The consequences of this may include difficulties in understanding National Curriculum requirements (particularly with regard to uses and applications of mathematics) and in being able to put these into practice. Teachers may also experience difficulties in assessing pupils. The particular skills needed to understand children's development in the processes of mathematical thinking may be assumed to be far harder to acquire than the skills required to administer a test to judge children's acquisition of facts. The development of such skills can only be inhibited by a lack of experience of the processes in teachers' personal learning of mathematics.

There has been some evidence to suggest that standards in mathematics are lower than they should be. It certainly seems true to say that whatever the aims might be for teaching mathematics, whether as a useful tool for everyday life or as an intellectual discipline, these aims are not being met. Attempts to define and prescribe a curriculum in law have not had the desired effect, at least in part because it has not addressed the fundamental problem of how mathematics is learnt and therefore how it should be taught. The National Curriculum, with the exception of the programmes of study for using and applying, is a list of content that could be said to reaffirm mathematics as a body of established rules and procedures to be learnt. The content might be broader and more articulately stated than previous curricula but if teachers are to improve their teaching of mathematics without dependency on teaching rules and procedures they need to unpick the meaning of mathematics and understand the essential processes of mathematical thought and action. Attempts to redefine the knowledge content will only change one scheme for another.

It would seem that school mathematics has reinforced the static model for educating today's learners – learners who are ultimately the teachers of tomorrow. This model appears to deny children the opportunity to see themselves as autonomous mathematical thinkers who can take delight in mathematical discovery and who can use mathematics as a resource to interpret and solve problems in their daily and working lives. In the case of the latter, the demand for creative mathematical problem solvers in the world of employment is likely to grow rather than diminish and employees who cannot use their mathematical knowledge, no matter how extensive it is, are unlikely to be of great service in an increasingly complex technological environment. The uses and applications of mathematics, its cultural and social perspectives, its history and development and its essential creativity are essential elements of the curriculum if children are to acquire genuine and effective understanding that will enable them to achieve success in school and that will serve them in their adult lives.

Reflection

Consider your own feelings about mathematics. Is it a 'source of delight and wonder' or a subject you dislike? Reflect on the origins of your feelings.

This chapter began with some examples of attitudes of adults towards mathematics. Cockcroft suggested that attitudes have a pervasive and far reaching effect on children's learning of the subject and that positive attitudes supported learning whilst negative attitudes not only inhibited learning but could be very difficult to change 'and very often persist into adult life and affect choice of job'. The teachers who attempt to bring innovation to their teaching of mathematics may well find that they can bring about real and worthwhile change in what the subject means to their pupils. I would suggest that central to this process is a commitment to developing motivation, enthusiasm and interest in their personal attitudes as well as in the pupils that they teach. Any attempt to restructure the way mathematics is taught needs to acknowledge that there may be more to good teaching and effective learning than the nature and purposes of the subject matter. Mathematics needs to be recognised for its usefulness and practical applications and its potential for creative and imaginative thought but it also needs to be viewed by children, parents and educators as an enjoyable and worthwhile activity.

Note

1   The first volume of the Nuffield Mathematics Project *I Do, and I Understand*, was dedicated 'with gratitude and permission' to Jean Piaget.

References

AHMED, A. (1987) *Better Mathematics – A Curriculum Development Study*, London: HMSO.

ASKEW, M., BROWN, M., RHODES, V., JOHNSON, D. and WILIAM, D. (1997) *Effective Teachers of Numeracy*, London: King's College.

COCKCROFT, W. H. (1982) *Mathematics Counts*, London: HMSO.

DES (1991) *Mathematics at Key Stages 1 and 3*, London: HMSO.

DES (1991) *Mathematics at Key Stages 1 and 2*, London: HMSO.

DES (1992) *Mathematics: Key Stages 1, 2 and 3*, London: HMSO.

DES (1994) *Mathematics at Key Stages 1, 2, 3 and 4*, London: HMSO.

ERNEST, P. (1991) *The Philosophy of Mathematics Education*, London: Falmer Press.

GRIFFITHS, H. B. and HOWSON, A. G. (1974) *Mathematics: Society and Curricula*, Cambridge: Cambridge University Press.

Howson, A. G. (1982) *A History of Mathematics Education in England*, Cambridge: Cambridge University Press.

Mathematical Association (1955) *The Teaching of Mathematics in Primary Schools*, London: G Bell & Sons.

Mogford, B. (1966) 'Active Learning, from The Nuffield Mathematics Project Bulletin 3' in Mansfield, D. E. (Ed) *Mathematical Forum*, Edinburgh: W. & R. Chambers.

National Numeracy Project (1998) *Framework for Numeracy (Draft)*, London: DfEE.

NCC (1989) *Mathematics Non-statutory Guidance*, York: National Curriculum Council.

Piaget, J. (1941) *The Child's Conception of Number* (translated by Gattegno, C. and Hodgeson, F. M., 1952), London: Routledge & Kegan Paul.

Reynolds, D. and Farrell, S. (1996) *Worlds Apart?* London: HMSO.

Schools Council (1965) *Mathematics in Primary Schools, Curriculum Bulletin No. 1*, London: HMSO.

Sharpe, R. (1995) 'Teaching teachers mathematics', *Action Researcher: Issue 3*, Summer 1995, pp. 7–8, Bournemouth: Hyde Publications.

Sharpe, R. (1998) *The Use of Commercial Schemes in the Teaching of Mathematics*, MPhil Thesis, Bristol: University of the West of England.

Williams, E. M. and Shuard, H. (1994) *Primary Mathematics Today*, London: Longman Group.

Chapter 7	New approaches: the National Numeracy Project, the 'Numeracy Hour' and the teaching of mathematics

Ruth Sharpe

❝ *Properly planned and funded evaluations should be a feature of curriculum developments in the future so that succeeding curriculum developments can build on strengths and address the weaknesses of previous innovations.*

(Askew, Brown, Rhodes, Johnson and William, pp. 43–44)

❝ *The National Curriculum programmes of study describe what must be taught in each key stage.*

After extensive consultation, a framework has been developed to illustrate how the programmes of study can be planned and taught in each year.

(National Numeracy Project, 1998, p. 7)

❝ *I am sending it to you with a considerable health warning. Schools taking part in the National Numeracy Project have been using the material since January 1997 and it is still being evaluated. We have already made revisions and will continue to do so.*

(Anita Straker, Director, National Numeracy Project, September 1997, see National Numeracy Task Force, 1998)

Background to the National Numeracy Project

The teaching of mathematics has been the subject of debate since the beginning of statutory schooling. Despite widespread initiatives and centrally funded development projects, mathematics appears to remain as Cockcroft suggested 'a difficult subject to learn and to teach'. Although the National Curriculum initiated widespread change by setting out a statutory curriculum for teachers to follow, research and inspection evidence seemed to suggest that, despite these changes, teaching in many cases remained inadequate and children's achievements were unsatisfactory.

The Department for Education and Employment set up the National Numeracy Project in September 1996 in response to these concerns. It was intended to support and inform the Numeracy Task Force, which in turn had the aim of ensuring that 75% of all 11-year-olds 'achieve at least level 4 in the National Curriculum Tests for mathematics' (introduction to the draft *Framework*, March 1998). More specifically it was set up with the aim of raising standards in line with national expectations in those schools taking part in the project. It was central to the government's National Numeracy Strategy and was supported by government and LEA funding for both teacher development and the provision of resources. As a consequence of the research, the project produced detailed guidance on planning and teaching the National Curriculum programmes of study. This guidance formed the *National Numeracy Project Framework* document (hereafter the *Framework*) and its main features were the promotion of interactive whole class teaching and the improvement of the management in schools of numeracy through 'target setting linked to systematic action planning, monitoring and evaluation'. Although a research project initially, the Numeracy Project, like the Literacy Project, became an approach to teaching mathematics that teachers seemed to feel they were expected to adopt. The recommendations of the Numeracy Task Force (1998) included the advice that OFSTED is to 'ensure that inspection of schools include evaluation of their implementation of the National Numeracy Strategy' (p. 58) and that 'all classes in mainstream primary schools [are] to devote a daily timetabled lesson of between 45 minutes and one hour . . . to mathematics . . .' (p. 52). It seemed to many teachers that the *Framework* was obligatory and that inspection would 'police' its implementation.

The *Framework* is intended to cover the whole of the National Curriculum for mathematics (not just number) and prescribes objectives for teaching for each year of the primary school from reception to Year 6. A central component of the *Framework* is the so-called Numeracy Hour. Each class is expected to have daily lessons of mathematics of about 45 minutes at Key Stage 1 and 50 minutes to an hour at Key Stage 2. The lesson typically starts with 10 minutes or so of oral work or mental calculation, including rehearsal of 'number bonds' and times tables, followed by 'the main teaching activity' and a plenary session. The emphasis throughout is on 'direct teaching' which is described as 'oral and interactive'. Direct teaching is defined as being comprised of five elements: demonstration, explanation, questioning, discussion and evaluation of pupils' responses, and direction. The *Framework* document advises that 'you should aim to spend close to 100 per cent of your time in direct teaching and questioning of either the whole class or a group of pupils'.

The teaching approach is clearly intended to respond to the concerns raised in Chapter 6, particularly removing the element of unproductive individualised learning highlighted in the two Case Studies. It also reflects the Connectionist orientation with an emphasis on challenging children's thinking, identifying and responding to errors and misconceptions and making explicit the connections between mathematical ideas. The objectives for teaching are set at the highest ability group in the class with the aim of narrowing the gap between the highest and lowest attainers and stretching the abilities of all children.

The *Framework* document: strengths

A particular strength of the project lies in its focus on involving children in collaborative whole class and group activities. Such collaboration can enable children to develop their skills in communicating mathematical ideas and to benefit from the broader experiences offered by working with others. Children working individually through work cards or textbooks is discouraged through this approach. In conjunction with this, the focus on discussion and talk is encouraging. Straker (1993) stated that:

> *Mathematical discussion is an activity in its own right as well as a valuable part of other tasks. Its purpose is to clarify and communicate ideas. . . . Sadly children are frequently expected to write mathematics before they have learned to imagine and discuss, and those who do not easily make connections are offered more pencil and paper work instead of the vital talk and discussion. Yet in other subjects it would be unthinkable to ask children to write what they cannot say.*
>
> (p. 1)

There is an emphasis in the *Framework* on children recording as a consequence of mental and oral work rather than undertaking such work for its own sake. Further, it would appear that discussion is not only intended to be a means of clarifying and communicating ideas but also a means of assessing children and identifying difficulties and misconceptions. In the case of the latter it seems wholly appropriate that mistakes or misunderstandings should be dealt with in the first instance by talking to children about what they have done. Cockcroft had much to say about discussion, recommending that mathematics lessons for all ages should include opportunities for discussion between teachers and pupils and the pupils themselves (para. 243).

A further strength of the project lies in its emphasis on the development of children's methods and strategies for doing calculations. Providing children with the means to develop their own models and building on these is surely more productive than teaching them to remember an algorithm that they may only partially understand and easily forget. Research (see for example, Aubrey, 1993; Hughes, 1987) suggests that very young children often have idiosyncratic methods for calculation which can be quite sophisticated and that the teaching of standard algorithms may inhibit the development of these.

One aspect of the numeracy hour itself that seems particularly useful, and one which many teachers probably already include in their teaching, is the plenary session. Children have the opportunity to share their work with the rest of the class and the teacher has the opportunity to focus the main issues, highlight aspects of the work and prepare the ground for future progress. I have found in my own teaching that if children are aware that they will be expected to let others know what they have been doing then it seems to give them a greater sense that their work is valued and a sense of purpose in what they are doing.

I believe that many teachers welcome the support the *Framework* gives them for their planning and management. The clearly stated objectives, suggestions for lessons, advice and guidance on delivery are thorough and comprehensive. Guidance is not only given about the objectives to be met, differentiation, group size and timing, but also on the arrangement of the furniture. It would seem as if the issues for which support is offered are those that have arisen during the implementation of the *Framework* in the project schools. The quotation at the beginning of this chapter endorses that supposition as it suggests that the work is developmental and that the *Framework* is, at least in intention, flexible and responsive to change. This is to be welcomed.

The *Framework* document: some concerns

The suggestion above that the *Framework* is a flexible one is, I believe, as it should be. No single method or approach is going to withstand the potential variety and breadth of current and future circumstances. As I suggested in

Chapter 6, the mathematics curriculum has responded to the changing needs of society and there can be little doubt that change and development will continue into the twenty-first century. Research, too, will continue to make new insights into how children learn mathematics and how it can be most effectively taught. A static and rigid model for teaching would, I believe, very quickly become redundant.

Evidence of the success of the project in the original schools was persuasive and certainly suggested measured gains in children's achievements. Despite this, it needs to be acknowledged that the success of the project in its preliminary stages may not guarantee that all teachers adopting the approach will be able to achieve the same results. Educational projects have a history of being successful in those schools committed to the aims and involved in the original research. It is not always possible to analyse precisely what is responsible for the success. It could be simply the increased attention given to mathematics in the schools concerned, the support of in-service courses or the commitment of the headteacher that was responsible for the measured gains in achievement rather than any particular pedagogy or approach. This is not to say that the approach is not valuable or that there is insufficient data to warrant a commitment to changing practice. It does mean that if the lessons are to be learnt from previous experiences and if mathematics teaching is to move forward, teachers need to continue to be vigilant and reflective about their personal practice and be wary of adopting the structure of new initiatives without thinking for themselves about the underlying processes and philosophy. It would be naïve to imagine that there is a single solution to the difficulties some teachers have in teaching mathematics, no matter how well researched or well founded that solution appears to be. It would also be irresponsible for teachers to take on such an innovation without being willing to analyse critically their practice in the context of any changes they are making.

In this context the most critical challenge to the numeracy project must lie in the use of prescription as a means of improving practice. Kelly (1989) argued that there are difficulties with approaches to curriculum development that are externally planned and determined. He suggested that in these circumstances there is a 'wide gap between the ideas of a project held by its central planners and the realities of its implementation . . . in the classroom by teachers' (p. 128) and that teachers need to be personally committed to innovation if it is to be effective. It could be argued that the numeracy project involved practising teachers and gave them the opportunity to share the original aims of the central planners through the considerable in-service support to project schools. However, this was not necessarily the case for schools adopting the *Framework*. Ahmed (1987) argued that teaching itself should be viewed as a researching activity and that where 'research is embedded in teachers' own experiences it holds more meaning and credibility for them' (p. 42). He suggested that 'no imported curriculum development exercise can be effective without working commitment and teacher involvement' (p. 43). and that

> to succeed on a wide scale, dissemination must be firmly rooted in the personal experiences of teachers in their classroom. Hence it must depend on personal contact based on shared experience . . . If curriculum development is to be widespread, successful and sustained, money must be made available to release teachers on a regular basis. (p. 45)

The fact that the numeracy project *Framework* document was underpinned by authoritative research and that there were teachers who were involved in that research did not necessarily make the research findings any more accessible to those teachers who did not have the opportunity to share them. I would suggest that a minimum requirement for the success of the project is to have the level of support sustained for all teachers and all teachers given the opportunity to share the project's philosophy and aims.

One issue that could become problematical with the implementation of the *Framework* is the volume and level of the detail of the written guidance offered to teachers. The precise direction on every aspect of planning, management, organisation and assessment in the *Framework* has been useful to many teachers. However, there is the possibility that the level of detail could be counter-productive or camouflage the need for genuine teacher development and in-service support. Where teachers understand and share the philosophy and principles that underpin the *Framework*, such advice is unnecessary and might even be considered demeaning to teacher professionalism. The development of negative attitudes in the teachers that use the materials is unlikely to be conducive to success. On the other hand, if teachers do not understand or share this philosophy and these principles then they may need more than the written document and the in-service support that an individual school is able to offer to put the *Framework* into practice. Such teacher development is likely to need sustained long-term in-service training that may be beyond the capacity of many schools to provide. The initial proposals were that most schools would have three days of INSET training for the mathematics co-ordinator, the headteacher and one other teacher. There was provision for 'weak' schools to have additional in-service support with the same individuals attending for five days of INSET training but there was no initial funding available on the scale of, say, the post-

Cockcroft initiatives that began in 1985. For the majority of teachers the level of support (other than the *Framework* document) was dependent on what the school could provide.

With any consideration of approaches to teaching the primary concern must be the effect on children's learning. Whilst the National Numeracy Project demonstrated measurable gains in children's achievements overall, these gains have been achieved in a relatively short time span and with a particular focus on number and computation. At the time of writing, long term gains have yet to be measured and the wider implications of the kind of learning that has taken place have not been analysed. There are perhaps three issues that you may wish to think about in this context.

The first is to do with the permanency of the gains achieved. If learning is to be sustained it will surely have to be the kind of learning that is built on genuine conceptual understanding. It is certainly the intention of the *Framework* to ensure that this is the case but if gains are to be measured in terms of the acquisition of facts and skills that may be likely, lack of understanding could be masked by an apparent ability to perform under test conditions. The statutory requirement for the assessment and reporting of pupil achievement and progress together with associated concerns with league tables and teacher competency may result in an anxiety to produce quantifiable evidence in terms of reliably measurable outcomes. Steinburg, Haymore and Marks (1985) suggested that a consequence of such anxiety may be to induce instrumentalist teaching that is characterised by rote learning tasks and the performance of algorithmic problem solving. This could arguably reinforce mechanistic perceptions of the content and delivery of school mathematics and further reduce the desire or the need to either teach the processes of mathematical thinking or secure further professional development. The impact of this on children's learning could be profound.

The second issue is to do with the validity of the learning, particularly in the long term. Whilst most would agree that it is desirable for children to meet the objectives given both in the *Framework* and the National Curriculum there are other aspects of mathematical learning that I believe should not be ignored. Central to these is the development of good work habits and the fostering of positive attitudes.

Good work habits, according to HMI (1984) include the ability to work imaginatively, creatively and flexibly and I would argue that the *Framework* provides more scope for the development of these attributes than most of the popular commercial schemes. However, providing opportunities for children to be innovative and independent thinkers, whilst at the same time maintaining the development of focused objectives, is undoubtedly a challenging task. It is nevertheless an essential one if the learners of today are to be able to respond and contribute to cultural developments and their own and society's needs in the twenty-first century.

The development of positive attitudes is, as Cockcroft argued, an essential component of effective mathematical development. Cockcroft maintained that every mathematics lesson developed a child's attitudes towards mathematics and that

 positive attitudes assist the learning of mathematics; negative attitudes not only inhibit learning but . . . very often persist into adult life and affect choice of job. (*Mathematics Counts*, 1982, para. 345)

The *Framework* does not in itself of course preclude or prohibit the development of positive attitudes but they are not mentioned nor are they cited as important objectives. The focus of the *Framework* is on achieving targets in terms of the development of knowledge, skills and understanding in National Curriculum terms. It could be argued that it is the job of teachers to develop positive attitudes whilst delivering the mathematics curriculum but the lack of reference to such a central issue may have the effect of demeaning its status. It is surely not enough that children achieve good results in Key Stage 2 Standard Assessment Tests. They need also to acquire an attitude towards mathematics that fosters fascination, motivation, pleasure and enjoyment if they are to continue to study the subject to A level and beyond. You might wish to consider what would happen if, despite being able to get good marks in tests, children learn to dislike the subject and have the feelings of fear and panic described by parents in Chapter 6.

The third issue in relation to children's learning is the need to address the different ways children make sense of mathematics. The *Framework* necessarily provides guidance on teaching. How children learn is much harder to describe with any certainty. Some children can have an almost intuitive grasp of complex and abstract ideas whereas some require much engagement with concepts, activities and materials before they can begin to make the connections that might truly be called understanding. This can be the case for children of the same age and even the same apparent ability. I do not believe the way children learn can be predicted, much less controlled. In many circumstances a teacher may not even know what a child is learning or be suddenly overwhelmed by evidence of an unexpected leap of understanding. For me this is what makes teaching so complex and so interesting. The clear hierarchy of year by year objectives has perhaps the potential to undermine flexible approaches to the different pathways that different pupils travel in order to achieve their full potential. HMI (1984) maintained that 'mathematical learning does not take place in a completely pre-determined sequence and any assumption that it does can seriously stunt pupils' progress' (p. 36). The following Case Study illustrates this point by highlighting the different ways in which some young children responded to the request of 'find the biggest number'.

Case Study 1

Children's insights

It is the beginning of the autumn term and the children in a reception class are sitting on the carpet at the beginning of the morning session. They are all in their first week of school. A visiting teacher is taking the class and wants to use the computer programme 'Counter',[1] to see how much these 4-year-olds know about numbers. The children watch as the numbers on the screen count, starting at 0 and going up in ones. When it reaches 15, she stops the programme and invites the children to say what they have seen. Some children call out some of the numbers seen, some say that the numbers were going 'up' and some say, 'it's counting'. One child says he saw the number 20 and there is some disagreement. Abigail says, 'It's not got that far.'

The teacher continues the programme and the numbers reach 20. She stops it again and after some more discussion asks the children what number they think it would go up to. Most seem to think it could go up to 100 – this seems to be a number that interests them – a milestone in numbers. Hannah says she thinks it would be 74 – because that is a really big number. The teacher speculates as to why this number is important. Perhaps a grandparent has just celebrated a 74th birthday? Alan says he thought it would be 101. When asked how he knows that, he replies, ''cos a hundred is the biggest number I know and I bet it gets bigger than that!'

The teacher runs the programme on and as the numbers get nearer to a hundred the excitement is tangible. The children might not be able to 'read' the numbers, but they have a good idea of their magnitude. The teacher stops the computer at 101 and asks the biggest number question again. Jamie says it should get to the number that fills the screen, which is 'probably about a million'. Hattie says, 'It will be a hundred million zillion trillion' and Melanie says, 'It's the everlasting number.' The children seem impressed with this last comment so Melanie is asked to explain what she means. 'Numbers', she says, 'go on and on and you never get to the end but if you did that's what it would be.' Michael says, 'It will get to a googol.' Again there is a show of interest from the children and he is asked to explain what a googol is. 'It's the biggest number there is and it's really, really big,' he tells them.

The teacher continues with the programme asking the children to watch what is happening, exploring patterns, making predictions. After about 15 minutes she re-sets the counter to zero and asks the children to predict how long it might take to get to their biggest numbers. She is particularly interested in Michael's response. He says, with great confidence, 'It will take until lunch-time.' The teacher leaves the programme running whilst the children get on with other activities.

At lunchtime the number on the computer is almost at 3000. 'Oh, no, it's miles off,' says Michael. He is invited to change his prediction. 'I can't work it out,' he admits, 'it's so big. But it's definitely after lunch.'

A week later the teacher is in the school again. Michael comes up to her with a huge grin. 'I know what a googol is,' he says. 'It's ten to the power of a hundred and that's a 1 with a hundred zeros and it would take you millions and millions of years to get there.' Michael is four years and nine months old.

The *Framework* document acknowledges that the experiences of young children are varied and that teaching should build on this by promoting discussion about numbers and how they are used. The Case Study above illustrates this but it also suggests the possibility that the next stage of development may be very different for at least some of the children in the class. Whilst accepting that providing individual programmes for each child is unrealistic, the *Framework* appears to advocate the development of the same programme for everyone, regardless of what they have achieved, what they already know or, perhaps more importantly, where their interests and enthusiasms lie. The aim, I suggested earlier, is to 'narrow the gap' between the highest and lowest attainers. Whilst this might make curriculum delivery easier, it may not help children to be innovative and creative in their thinking or encourage independence and flexibility of thought. It might have the effect of producing competent calculators at Year 6 but this could be at the expense of inhibiting the development of future resourceful and inventive mathematicians.

Enquiry task 1

1   A googol is 10 to the power 100 or a 1 with a hundred zeros. Starting at 0 and counting one number per second how long would it take you to reach a googol? Consider the strategies you use to solve this problem. Consider the place of the calculator in work of this kind. What could be the next stage of development for Michael?
2   Ask the children in your class some 'big number' questions. You might just ask them for the biggest number they can think of or what is the biggest (smallest) number they can put on a calculator. You could also give them a 'counting challenge', e.g. How many blades of grass are there in a field? How many bricks did it take to build the school? How old are you in weeks, (hours, minutes, and seconds)?
3   Record their responses and identify any differences in children's thinking and understanding.
4   Identify what you could do next to capitalise on what they know.

One final point for reflection is the requirement of the *Framework* to use time available for mathematics in a particular way. I suggested above that the detail of the *Framework* could be considered both a help and a hindrance. This may be particularly true in the context of the management of teachers' and children's time. The daily 'hour' of close to 100% direct teaching could act as a constraint as well as a benefit. Whilst it is capable of really focusing both the teacher and the children into a routine of mathematical learning, practice and development, the requirement for some teachers and particularly some children that they should engage in productive sustained working may be wholly inappropriate. I am thinking in particular of classrooms where the social and emotional needs of the children may have a higher priority than their need to do well in SATs. You might wish to consider if the price for achieving academic targets in mathematics, at the expense of children's other needs, is a price that should be paid. The idea of maximum efficiency in learning may be an attractive one but it could also be an expensive one in terms of children's (and teachers') well-being.

Implementing the *Framework*

In raising the issues above, I do not intend to suggest that the numeracy hour or any other part of the *Framework* should be rejected. Teachers continue to have the responsibility for their pupils' progress and development and must continue to respond professionally to the task of teaching. This means that the implementation of any new initiative needs to be viewed not as a solution to the problems and complexities of teaching and learning but as a source of further classroom research and reflection about what is effective and appropriate. In this context what may be needed is a move away from those practices that have seemed to fail in the past and a fresh look at those practices which appear to be more successful. The success of the project in the original schools needs, perhaps, to be the starting point for future development by capitalising on its strengths and improving practice through identifying those aspects that are less effective. The following Case Study illustrates the difficulties of one particular teacher in implementing the numeracy hour with the intention of providing some material for reflecting on how such difficulties might be overcome.

Case Study 2

Janet's Numeracy Hour

Janet is a Year 1 class teacher in a large rural primary school. She is not an enthusiastic mathematics teacher and her teaching before adopting the numeracy hour relied heavily on home-produced work cards based on a commercial scheme. She is not the mathematics co-ordinator although the co-ordinator and head of the school are enthusiastic and supportive. She is aware of the format of the numeracy project, is well-organised and has good classroom management skills. Children are invariably on task in her room and she has clear expectations for the children's behaviour. The lesson begins with 15 minutes of whole class work. Janet first explains that the children are going to learn 'doubles'. She explains that a double is twice another number and that they are very useful. She demonstrates with counting cubes showing that a tower of four and another tower of four makes a tower of eight. She shows several similar examples of this. She then makes some towers of four, six and eight cubes and asks the children what doubles they might represent. The children that answer make the correct response. She then says there are some numbers that are not doubles. She makes a tower of 7 and shows it to the children. She asks them if it is a double. Jimmy replies that it is double 3½. Janet says, 'No, dear, it is not a double.' Janet then uses a collection of attractively laminated cards with sums on them, which she has taken to using at the introductory sessions. She uses these in the form of an oral test, choosing cards at random and presenting them to children to 'answer the sum'. She has decided to use those with 'doubles' and 'near doubles' on them for this lesson. She wants the children to answer quickly so that they will be good at 'instant recall' but this seems to make some of the children nervous. There are some requests to use the toilet and one child seems as if he is trying to hide behind the child in front. Some children seem to guess the answers whilst others resort to fingers – she tells them they are not to do either of these things. Some children get the answers right and some do not. Those that get the wrong answers are asked to explain how they got them, as Janet knows that she must challenge 'errors and misconceptions' but the usual response is a shrug of the shoulders. She tries asking those who get the answers right to explain what they have done and their responses include 'I did it in my brain', 'I just did it' and one child who says, 'my mum told me'.

Janet then sets the children to work in groups where they have work cards that are differentiated according to the ability of the child. The lower ability children are given some structured apparatus to help them. Janet spends her time keeping the children on task and encouraging them to finish. Five minutes before playtime she stops the children and asks them to put their work on her table and tidy up their equipment. Drawing the class together again she tells them they have been learning about doubles and they've all worked very hard. She has made it clear in discussion that she sees no point to the plenary session as it uses up work time and time to tidy up. In any case, she is satisfied that all the children get feedback when she marks their work.

Reflection

Why do you think the children might be feeling nervous during this session? What effect might this have on their learning and their attitudes towards mathematics? What would you do to encourage the children to think about the strategies they use?

In the Case Study above, Janet's practice is largely unchanged by the introduction of the Numeracy Hour. She is able to deliver it efficiently using all her considerable management skills. Her view of mathematics is predicated on a belief that she has to teach a set of rules and skills. Under these circumstances the learning of traditional sums through an algorithmic approach has been substituted for the learning of new sums – in this case learning doubles. Using doubles in calculation might be a strategy that numerate children use. This does not necessarily mean that telling children about doubles or telling them that they are useful will make them numerate. Perhaps they need to see the sense and purpose of them for themselves. Janet's questioning of the children is 'closed' and as this is the format they are used to it seems likely that their unwillingness or inability to discuss answers may be driven by a perceived need to provide the answer the teacher wants rather than to reveal their own thinking. The dismissal of the $3\frac{1}{2}$ answer is evidence of this. The session reveals little and makes little use of what the children already know or have learnt during their time on the carpet or in their main activity time. Janet relies heavily on explaining concepts to the children. It seems to me that the difficulty with this is that understanding the explanation may be conceptually harder than understanding the mathematics. One solution might be to provide children with experiences that include, in this case, the manipulation of doubles in calculations and using this as the basis for inviting children to explain to you what they are doing.

Whilst visiting a Year 2 class, I observed some children doing addition calculations that involved answers between 10 and 20. They had been given cubes and had been told to count out the number of cubes for each number in the sum and then count the cubes altogether to get the answer. I noticed that most were getting the answer 'wrong' and this seemed to be entirely due to miscounting the cubes. I asked the children to ignore the cubes and just do in their heads some of the sums. One sum was 7 + 9. The children responded almost instantly with 16 and when I asked them how they had done it one child told me he had in fact done the sum as double eight because he knew that answer and knew it was the same. Another child said she had made the 9 into 10 and the seven into 6 because she could do that sum easily. Of course, both these responses are correct and appropriate and demonstrate how children (and, of course, adults) use the mental resources they have to solve problems of this kind. What teaching can do is make the different approaches explicit. This not only validates them but should also enable children to have within their experiences a range of different approaches that they can draw on as and when they need them. Simply 'explaining' doubles as the method to use and then getting the children to apply the explanation is not likely to lead many of them to add this particular strategy to their repertoire. *The Non-statutory Guidance for Mathematics* suggests that:

 The teacher's job is to organise and provide the sorts of experiences which enable pupils to construct their own understanding of mathematics, rather than simply communicate the ways in which they themselves understand the subject. (NCC, 1989, p. C2, para. 2.2)

Enquiry task 2

1   Take a closed question e.g. What is 7 + 9? and make it open (e.g. 'I'm thinking of two numbers that make 16, what do you think they might be?')
2   Give the question to the children in your class. Ask, 'can you do it another way?' and 'how did you know that?'
3   Devise a game or activity that uses doubles (e.g. a simple board 'race game' where some squares allow you to double the next throw of the dice).
4   List as many things as you can that you could do to encourage the children to give you feedback in a plenary session. Consider how you would use this as an opportunity to develop their thinking further.

The following Case Study illustrates a more successful 'Numeracy Hour'.

Case Study 3

Linda's Numeracy Hour

The lesson was with a mixed Year 5/6 class in a large primary school. The teacher, Linda, was an experienced practitioner and the mathematics co-ordinator. She said that she felt that the way she taught had not changed particularly since introducing the 'hour' in her classroom. On this occasion she was working with another teacher's class with the class teacher observing her. The aim was to develop practice in the school through modelling the approach. The class had always used a commercial scheme, working individually, and there was a wide spread of ability that included Dean who had a statement of special educational need because of learning difficulties.

The lesson began by asking all the children if they knew what 'sums' were. There were some groans in the class but they agreed that sums were familiar to them. Linda told the children that they were going to be doing sums but that whereas they normally would have to work out the answer she was going to ask them to work out the question. This caused some amusement and there were children who clearly thought this was going to be very easy. Linda then wrote on the board a large number 10. She told them this was the answer, could they think of the sum? The class was silent for a moment before one child asked if it was 5 + 5. She wrote that down. The class seemed visibly to relax and the answers then came swiftly; initially all the pairs of numbers that added to 10 and then, as children gained in confidence, subtraction, multiplication and division sums were offered. Linda began by acting as scribe for the answers but after a short time began to challenge the children's responses and directly encourage an awareness of patterns, relationships and structures. She did this by grouping the responses in similar categories (addition, multiplication and so on) as she wrote them on the board and also by using a response as the start to a pattern. For example, $10 - 0$, $11 - 1$, $12 - 2$ etc. asking the children to say what they noticed and what they could predict. One interesting pattern began with 1×10, 2×5. There was a good deal of discussion before $3 \times 3\frac{1}{3}$ was agreed as the next sum in the series. One child had suggested 3.33 recurring but this, they argued, would only give 9.99 recurring, not 10. The next sums were given as $4 \times 2\frac{1}{2}$ and 5×2. 6 caused much discussion and speculation until $6 \times 1\frac{2}{3}$ was agreed. She asked if there was anyone who did not understand this. No-one put their hands up. 'Does that mean', she asked, 'that I can ask anyone to explain it to me?' There was a brief look of anxiety from the class until Daniel said he did not understand. She congratulated Daniel for telling her this and then asked if there was someone who could explain it to him. Several children had a go using a variety of techniques – modelling, making pictures and so on. Linda asked Daniel once more if he understood and when he said he did she asked him to explain it to someone else who did not understand. When the next child understood they in turn explained it to someone else. Understanding was confirmed by the way that the children were quickly able to find the next three sums.

All this took about 20 minutes. Linda then told them that they were now going to work on their own with a partner. She said she wanted them to find as many new '10' patterns as they could. As they worked she moved round the class questioning and challenging children asking them to explain patterns, change their rule, make predictions and asking 'what would happen if?' types of questions. Particularly interesting examples were written on the board for all the children to see. This included Dean's offering of $1 + 1 + 1 + 1 + 1 + 1 + 1 + 1 + 1 + 1$, $2 + 2 + 2 + 2 + 2$, $3\frac{1}{3} + 3\frac{1}{3} + 3\frac{1}{3}$. This was not only a huge achievement for Dean, but also a clear indication that he had followed at least some of the discussion with the whole class.

About 15 minutes before the end, Linda stopped the class and invited them to say something about their patterns or findings. She asked particular children to explain what they had done, including Dean who confidently described his pattern. After each exposition she asked them what they were going to do next. At the end of the session some of the children were seen taking the work into the playground. The session had lasted nearly an hour and a half.

Linda explained after the lesson that her approach to teaching is predicated on a belief that the personal qualities of children should be developed first. An analysis of the lesson makes this clear. Her introduction is intended to put the children at ease and give them a sense of achievement before the lesson proper begins. She makes sure that the initial questions she asks are ones that they will be able to answer. All the children are able to make some contribution and she ensures that they do. She accepts every contribution and rewards the child who admits that he doesn't understand, inviting the class to build on this by generating explanations for each other. Nobody's contribution is rejected or ridiculed. She gains the children's trust and they are prepared to make an effort for her. Her manner is encouraging, positive and enthusiastic. When the children are asked to work independently she ensures that they can all make a start by leaving the examples on the board and suggesting that they may like to develop some of the patterns they have already made. This enables everyone to do something before she comes round to talk to the children. She values their continuing work through using their examples to put on the board and by encouraging them in their feedback afterwards. Her challenges to the children are genuine. She ensures that they are pushed to their limit and in doing so is effectively saying, 'I know how clever you are'. She also gives them time to answer. She calls this thinking time. The children are motivated, persistent and enthusiastic and gain a huge satisfaction from a sense of achievement.

Although developing personal qualities underpins her work with the children, there are other characteristics of Linda's work that make this session a success. She focuses on the children's strategies and explanations rather than on their answers, but she uses their answers as the beginning of a new enquiry by making links with other areas of knowledge both new and old. She avoids explanations and encourages the children instead to do any explaining for her. This enables the children to clarify their own understanding as well as being a means for developing the understanding of others. In the case of the former, I have often heard teachers say they have only understood some things themselves after having to explain it to children. It would seem that the process of articulating meaning strengthens conceptual understanding. In the case of the latter, and in my own teaching, I have often observed that children make more sense of an explanation offered by a peer than they do from one I have given them myself.

Enquiry task 3

1   Try out a simple starting point like the one in Linda's Case Study with your class – with younger children you might ask them what they know about the number 10. If you can, get someone to observe you or tape-record the session.

2   Assess your performance against your ability to develop children's attitudes towards mathematics. Did you enable the children to develop:
    fascination?
    interest and motivation?
    pleasure and enjoyment?
    an appreciation of the purpose, power and relevance of mathematics?
    satisfaction from sense of achievement?
    confidence?

3   Assess your ability to allow children 'thinking time'. Do you expect immediate responses or are you prepared to wait? If you do wait how long do you wait for?

4   Assess the children's development and plan the next stage. Include in your assessment the development of the personal qualities given above and suggest ways of improving those qualities that were lacking.

Conclusion

The National Numeracy Strategy and in particular the *Numeracy Framework Document* has the potential to be very effective both in terms of raising achievement and developing more successful practices in teaching mathematics. However, I believe that to make it effective will require the continuing development of the professional skills of the teachers using it. It is not in itself, nor can it be, a simple recipe for success any more than one particular rule for teaching children to calculate will make those children numerate. It could be argued that it is not *what* teachers do that counts so much as *how* they do it. I believe that central to the processes of effective teaching is the conviction that children and teachers have an entitlement to do well. This means they need to feel positive about what they are doing and feel that their work is valued and worthwhile. The key issues here for teachers include the desire to see teaching as a rewarding and interesting activity that provides them with the opportunities to reflect on those aspects of their work that they do well, to seize opportunities to move their practice forward and to continue to challenge assumptions about what helps children to learn. As Ahmed (1987) suggests, effective teaching is a researching activity that comes from critical reflection on personal practice. External research, analysis and debate necessarily inform such reflection. There are no single solutions to what will work in any particular set of circumstances but there are ways of moving forward that would appear to generate more effective approaches. In 1977, at the time of the so-called Great Debate about education (and especially mathematics education), Alistair McIntosh wrote that there was some consensus about what made 'good' mathematics teaching. He embodied this in eight principles that he spelt out as follows:

1   *Don't start formal work too early.*
2   *Use materials and start from practical experience.*
3   *Give children problems and freedom to find their own solution.*
4   *Children must have particular examples from which to generalise.*
5   *Go for relevance and the involvement of the child.*
6   *Go for reasons and understanding of processes. Never give mechanical rules.*
7   *Emphasise and encourage discussion by children.*
8   *Follow understanding with practice and applications.* (p. 95)

He added that:

It is doubtful if one child in a million has received a mathematical education consistently following these principles at every stage. Recent reports, and recent research, have done little more than expand on these rather aged methods, currently called 'progressive'. (ibid.)

It may be that little has changed since McIntosh wrote this. The *Numeracy Framework* has many of McIntosh's principles embedded in its philosophy. In keeping with the analysis presented in this chapter, I would suggest that we add to these the following:

1   Build on children's successes and achievements.
2   Focus on children's strategies and methods.
3   Listen to what children have to say about mathematics.
4   Develop open-ended questioning.
5   Develop positive attitudes and good work habits.
6   Develop personal enthusiasm for mathematics.
7   Reflect often and in depth.

I would like to think that whatever new initiatives are presented to teachers to support their work in the classroom, whatever new research reveals about children's learning, teachers will continue to challenge assumptions about their own work and develop a professional response to the task they are being asked to do. It is to be hoped that teachers will continue to find themselves able to question the practices they are being asked to employ and challenge the validity of anyone else's assumptions (including mine) with the aim of finding something better to replace them.

Note

1   'Counter' is on SLIMWAM II available from the Association of Teachers of Mathematics.

Annotated reading list

Askew, M. (1998) *Teaching Primary Mathematics*, London: Hodder and Stoughton. This book draws together ideas for teaching mathematics, particularly number, from research and work with teachers. The result is a 'unique blend of practical teaching advice underpinned by principles established by recent research'.

Askew, M., Brown, M., Rhodes, V., Johnson, D. and William, D. (1997) *Effective Teachers of Numeracy*, London: King's College.
A report of a study carried out for the TTA during 1995–96 by the School of Education, King's College, London, exploring the knowledge, beliefs and practices of those teachers recognised as being effective teachers of numeracy.

Atkinson, S. (ed) (1992) *Mathematics with Reason*, London: Hodder and Stoughton. This book explores the ways in which young children develop mathematical ideas and become 'mathematical thinkers'. It provides a theoretical perspective to mathematical development and includes ideas and activities based on research accounts.

Atkinson, S. (1996) *Developing a Scheme of Work for Primary Mathematics*, London: Hodder and Stoughton.
Whilst focusing on whole school schemes and policy documents, this book nevertheless will be useful for students and class teachers. It describes the essential elements of curriculum planning and discusses both pedagogic and practical issues.

Clarke, S. (1995) *Formative Assessment in Key Stage 1: Mathematics*, London: Hodder and Stoughton.
A practical book of assessment ideas and activities focused on the National Curriculum programmes of study at Key Stage 1.

Donaldson, M. (1985) *Children's Minds*, London: Fontana.
Donaldson explores and challenges the theories of Piaget and presents an alternative view of children's learning.

Ebbutt, S. and Straker, A. (1990) *Mathematics in Primary School*, London: Harcourt Brace and Jovanovich.
An examination of the nature of mathematics and children's learning with an exploration of teaching/learning styles, curriculum content and related issues e.g. the use of IT. It also includes some suggestions for topic-based activities in mathematics.

Harris, S. and Henkhuzen, Z. (1998) *Mathematics in Primary Schools*, Windsor, Berks: NFER.
A summary of current research into mathematics teaching in the primary school.

HAYLOCK, D. (1996) *Mathematics Explained for Primary Teachers*, London: Paul Chapman Publishers.
An explanation of concepts and processes of the mathematics taught in primary schools, with self-assessment exercises to test personal understanding.

HOPKINS, C., GIFFORD, S. and PEPPERELL, S. (1996) *Mathematics in the Primary Classroom: A Sense of Progression*, London: David Fulton.
A theoretical perspective of primary mathematics teaching.

HUGHES, M. (1987) *Children and Number*, Oxford: Blackwell.
This book explores Martin Hughes's research into how children learn about number (and why they might fail to). It examines the relationship between 'school maths' and children's understanding of mathematics and suggests ways in which the two might be linked more effectively.

LEWIS, A. (1996) *Discovering Mathematics with 4–7 year olds*, London: Hodder and Stoughton.
This accessible book gives sound guidance and practical advice in a theoretical context for teaching mathematics in the early years.

OFSTED (1997) *The Teaching of Number*, London: OFSTED Publications Centre.
A report describing and discussing OFSTED's findings regarding the teaching of number to Years 2 and 6 in 45 schools from three local education authorities.

ORTON, A. and FROBISHER, L. (1996) *Insights into Teaching Mathematics*, London: Cassell.
A guide to the meaning and application of concepts in mathematics with suggestions for work with children and self-assessment activities.

SCAA (1997) *The Teaching and Assessment of Number at KS 1–3*, London: SCAA.
This SCAA publication discusses theory and practice in relation to the teaching and learning of work in number. It examines recent and relevant research evidence which should inform practice.

STRAKER, A. (1993) *Talking Points in Mathematics*, Cambridge: CUP.
A practical and interesting guide to the role of language and discussion in the mathematics classroom.

THOMPSON, I. (1997) *Teaching and Learning Early Number*, Oxford: OUP.
Although focusing on early years, later years' students will also find this book useful in exploring the origins and early stages for developing number skills and understanding in the classroom.

Reports

COCKCROFT, W. *Mathematics Counts*, London: HMSO.
A report from the committee of enquiry chaired by W. Cockcroft into the teaching and learning of mathematics. This is a seminal text and makes a significant contribution to debates about mathematics education.

HMI (1984) *Mathematics from 5–16*, London: HMSO.
Based on the main findings of the Cockcroft Report, this report provides an analysis of aims, objectives, teaching styles, classroom approaches and assessment in mathematics teaching.

NCC (1989) *Non-statutory Guidance*, York: NCC.
This is essential reading. It links the findings of research to the Statutory Orders and suggests ways in which the National Curriculum might be implemented.

References

Ahmed, A. (1987) *Better Mathematics – A Curriculum Development Study*, London: HMSO.

Aubrey, C. (1993) 'An investigation of the mathematical knowledge and competencies which young children bring into school', *British Educational Research Journal*, **19**, 1, 1993, pp. 27–42.

HMI (1984) *Curriculum Matters: Mathematics from 5 to 16*, London: HMSO.

Kelly, A. V. (1989) *The Curriculum: Theory and Practice* (3rd Edition), London: Paul Chapman Press.

McIntosh, A. (1977) 'When will they ever learn', *Forum*, Summer, 1977.

National Numeracy Project (1998) *Framework for Numeracy, Reception to Year 6*, London: DfEE.

National Numeracy Task Force (1998) *The National Numeracy Strategy: Final Report*, London: HMSO.

Nuffield Mathematics Project (1967) *I Do and I Understand*, London: Chambers and Murray.

Piaget, J. (1941) *The Child's Conception of Number*, translated by Gattegno, C. and Hodgeson, F. M. (1952), London: Routledge and Kegan Paul.

Steinberg, R., Haymore, J. and Marks, R. (1985, April) *Teachers' Knowledge and Structuring Content in Mathematics*. Paper presented at the annual meeting of the American Educational Research Association, San Francisco.

Straker, A. (1993) *Talking Points in Mathematics*, Cambridge: Cambridge University Press.

Williams, E. M. and Shuard, H. (1994) *Primary Mathematics Today*, London: Longman Group.

Chapter 8

Development of the science curriculum

Gordon Guest and Keith Postlethwaite

Introduction

 If you want science you must begin by creating science teachers.

(Michael Faraday to the Royal Commission 1852 quoted in Hibbert, 1975)

The statement made by Faraday is still relevant. It implies three questions about the kind of science we want children to learn: what science is appropriate to children of various ages, cultures and religions; what is the role of a primary science teacher and is there a universal model or various models that apply to differing stages in education?

Various researchers and groups, as well as teacher educators have views on what science should be taught in primary schools[1]. The National Curriculum Council (1989) also presented views on how and why science should be taught. Not all of these views were in agreement. The British debate was informed by work in other countries, such as that by Osborne and Freyberg (1985) in New Zealand and Harnqvist and Burgens (1997). Peacock (1997) also discusses science from various national cultures and their educational traditions and values.

When I began teaching in rural Lincolnshire science was not a formal part of the curriculum. We focused mainly on nature study. This involved going on nature walks, drawing and naming some flowers and growing cress seeds. During my teaching career I have seen primary science develop (see Figure 8.1) from this kind of occasional 'Nature Study' and other activities such as 'making a lighthouse' to science as a core subject and an entitlement for all children with specified hours and content.

FIG 8.1
Twenty years of primary
science change and
development

1978	HMI Report on Primary Education, primary science was a cause for concern.
1983	HMI produced the Green Paper 'Science in Primary Schools': The Assessment of Performance Unit produced a report on children's achievement 'Science at age 11'.
1984	From 1984 to 1988 HMI produces a series of 16 booklets on the Curriculum 5 to 16. These covered a range of subjects and pastoral issues.
1985	The Department for Education (DFE) state primary school science was less effective than claimed. The DFE produced 'Science 5 to 16 a statement of policy'. Unlike the HMI 'Curriculum series', this was a clear indication of 'What would be taught in science' within primary and secondary schools.
1987	Science National Curriculum working group established.
1988	The first draft of the Science National Curriculum appeared with 22 attainment targets.
1989	The Science National Curriculum became a legal requirement, with 17 attainment targets. **All teachers must teach Science**. All children have an entitlement to receive science education to a satisfactory standard.'
1991	New Orders for science and mathematics. Both National Curriculum subjects re-written. Science reduced to four attainment targets.
1992	Art in the National Curriculum is written completing the foundation subjects.
1993	The Government reviews the National Curriculum. Sir Ron Dearing leads the review body. All the subjects are revised and the primary content in Key Stage 1 and Key Stage 2 is slimmed down.
1994	The 'Dearing Commission' completes the review of the Primary National Curriculum. Science retains four attainment targets but elements such as earth and space are removed.
1995	The New Revised National Curriculum appear in January 1995, although schools were beginning to use it from September 1994. Implementation was from September 1995. This was the third science curriculum change in six years.
1998	In July 1998 the Department for Education and Employment (DfEE) and the Qualifications and Curriculum Authority (QCA) produce a 'Scheme of work for science Key Stage 1 and Key Stage 2' along the lines of the literacy and numeracy hour. This set out six specific topics to be covered each year for each year group with time per topic, e.g. Year 2 Variation, nine hours.

This 20-year process charts a complete change in the delivery of the curriculum. From the 1970s when class teachers had personal autonomy over what they taught with the emphasis on individual learning to the late 1990s when content and teaching are prescribed by central government and teaching is more whole class based.

A review of the primary science curriculum development

The only subject requirement within the 1944 Education Act was religious education. How and what was taught in other subjects was left to the teacher's professional judgment. Britain moved from the austerity of the 1950s and rationing to a nation of full employment and rebuilding and expansion of education in the 1960s. This created the conditions for teachers and educators to experiment with a range of new approaches to educating children and for the influential Plowden Report of the late 60s that supported a child-centred approach to 'good primary practice'.

During the 1970s the 'Schools Council Science 5 to 13' (Schools Council, 1973) project produced a range of material to support teachers in developing science activities. In the 1990s these books are still drawn on in schools. This material considered children's scientific development to be linked to Piaget's conceptual stages of development. The theory was that some aspects of science were conceptually too difficult for children at particular ages. The approach established the idea of science as a practical subject that should begin in the infant school and develop through the junior school.

In 1978 Her Majesty's Inspectors (HMI, 1978) published an extensive report on primary education. It raised concerns about science not being broad enough, not progressively developing knowledge nor providing practical activities. It created a national impetus to develop science within primary education. A debate over process, content, and the type of curriculum developed drawing on the work of the Assessment and Performance Unit (1980 to 1984), and other researchers such as Wynne Harlen (1977), the Schools Council Progress in Learning Science Project (1973–1977) and Driver, Guesne and Tiberghein (1985). The debate over the emphasis of science, whether it should be on skills and processes or knowledge and concepts continues. The 1995 Curriculum suggests each are equally important, but the standards assessment tasks for 11-year-olds only assess knowledge.

The scene was now set for the development of a cohesive science curriculum programme for all children in primary schools. In July 1987 a science working party was established to write the Science National Curriculum, the first draft of which appeared in August 1988 with 22 attainment targets and programmes of study. This first draft curriculum included a few areas of science to be taught only within secondary schools and aspects of technology, the application of science, computer work, and the relationship of science to society. This curriculum encompassed a rich breadth, knowledge, skills, practical applications and ethical issues. The 1989 science curriculum was different. The attainment targets had been reduced from 22 to 17 and statements had been included for every level of attainment.

As the other foundation subjects began to be written and implemented and teachers saw the volume of subject knowledge in all curriculum areas that had to be covered there was criticism that in science the 17 attainment targets were too broad. This was partly due to schools feeling they were losing their autonomy and professional integrity, and partly due to a primary teaching workforce, largely untrained and unskilled in teaching primary science, anxious to reduce their delivery of science. The issue of teacher's ownership of science skills remains.

In 1991 the science curriculum was reduced to four programmes of study with four attainment targets. This format was continued in slimmed down form in the Dearing changes of 1994 to 1995 (see Figure 8.2), which also introduced a fifth programme of study.

1995 (Dearing) Programmes of Study (POS)
    POS 0   General (systematic enquiry, science in everyday life, the nature of scientific ideas, communication, health and safety)
    POS 1   Experimental and Investigative Science
    POS 2   Life Processes and Living Things
    POS 3   Materials and their Properties
    POS 4   Physical Processes

Attainment Targets were developed to match the Programmes of Study:
    AT1   Experimental and Investigative Science
    AT2   Life Processes and Living Things
    AT3   Materials and their Properties
    AT4   Physical Processes

Within each Attainment Target there are eight levels of achievement. These go from level 1 for infants to level 8 for 14-year-olds. These levels are used for assessing children's scientific knowledge and ability. Able children at Key Stage 2 would be expected to achieve level 5, those at Key Stage 1 level 3.

The National Curriculum was seen as beneficial to children because it provided for the first time a common curriculum framework. However this framework was clearly influenced by interest groups or changes in governmental thinking. The question as to whether the curriculum remains appropriate for all children remains.

The first Science National Curriculum was believed to include the best scientific practice and to be based on the values of the scientific community. The rewrite simplified the content for teachers.

In Figure 8.2 we present one aspect of the science curriculum, electricity, to illustrate how the requirements have changed between 1989 and 1999, a period of only 10 years.

In 1998, the Qualifications and Curriculum Authority (QCA) issued a scheme of work for science in primary schools covering Key Stage 1 and Key Stage 2. This lists six science topics a year for each year group and states the length of time that should be spent on each science topic in each half term. Many Key Stage 1 units have vertically grouped classes containing more than one year group. Centralised curriculum planning does not account for these variations. All primary schools will be expected to demonstrate that they either use the QCA science scheme or that they have a science scheme of work that is as effective.

Sir Josiah Mason, founder of Birmingham University, had a vision in 1872 that;

 All classes should be given the means of carrying on their scientific studies as completely and thoroughly as in the great science schools of the continent.

(Hibbert, 1975)

This vision is a reality at the start of the twenty-first century, with all children receiving a science education. Evidence from OFSTED indicates many areas of strength in science, although weaknesses are still identified.

 Standards in science have improved and the performance of English pupils in science now compares favourably with that of pupils in other countries . . . Attainment in science is overall similar to that in English but higher than that in mathematics.

(OFSTED, 1998)

Enquiry task I

Compare the three versions of the science curriculum related to electricity from 1989, 1995 and 1998, listed below.

What similarities and differences are there? Do the 1998 and the 1989 versions expect the same things from the class teacher?

FIG 8.2
National Curriculum
Enquiry tasks

The National Curriculum from 1989 to 1998: Electricity requirements

1989   National Curriculum   Attainment Target 11: Electricity and Magnetism

Key Stage 1   (Infants) Level 1
Know that many household appliances use electricity but that misuse could be dangerous

Level 2
Know that magnets attract certain materials but not others and can repel each other
Understand the danger associated with the use of electricity and know appropriate safety measures
Know that some materials conduct electricity well while others do not
Understand that a complete circuit is needed for an electrical device such as a bulb or buzzer to work

Key Stage 2   (Juniors) Level 4
Be able to construct simple electrical circuits

1995   Science National Curriculum   'Dearing Version'

Key Stage 1   (Infants)
- That many everyday appliances use electricity
- To construct simple circuits using batteries, wires, bulbs and buzzers
- That electrical devices will not work if there is a break in the circuit

Key Stage 2   (Juniors)
- A completed circuit including a battery or power supply, is needed to make electrical devices work
- How switches can be used to control electrical devices
- Ways of varying the current in a circuit to make bulbs brighter or dimmer
- How to represent series circuits by drawings and diagrams and how to construct series circuits on the basis of drawings and diagrams

1998   Qualifications and Curriculum Authority

Key Stage 1   (Infants)
- Everyday appliances use electricity; including things that light up, heat up, produce sounds and move
- That some devices use batteries which supply electricity, these can be handled safely
- To make connections in circuits to the positive and negative poles of the battery
- To make a complete circuit using a battery, wires and bulbs
- Explore how to make a bulb light, explaining what happened and using drawings to present results
- That an electrical device will not work if there is no battery or if there is a break in the circuit
- To make and test predictions about circuits that will work
- To make and record observations in drawings
- To explain what happened drawing on their knowledge of circuits.

Key Stage Two   (Juniors)

- That a circuit needs a power source
- That a complete circuit is needed
- That circuits powered by batteries can be used for investigations and experiment appliances connected to the mains must not [be used]
- That some materials are better conductors of electricity than others
- How to find out which materials allow electricity to pass through them
- To use results to draw conclusions about which materials conduct electricity
- That metals are good conductors of electricity, most other materials are not and that metals are used for cables and wires, plastics are used to cover wires and as covers for plugs and switches
- That a switch can be used to make or break a circuit, to turn things on or off
- To make predictions about the effect of including additional batteries in a circuit
- How to change the brightness of a bulb
- To make suggestions about what can be investigated and predictions about what will happen
- To plan to change one factor and keep others constant

International comparisons in 1997 (Burges, *TES*, May 1997) suggest English 11-year-olds were second only to Singapore in science achievement.

 In a recent international survey Year 5 pupils in England obtained mean scores which were exceeded by pupils in only three of the other 25 countries which took part. (OFSTED, 1998)

These results indicate improvement and success in the development and teaching of science in primary schools. Science is a core aspect of the Primary Curriculum, with all primary teachers involved in its delivery and all children experiencing science in the classroom. In 1998 at the time of these surveys, the teaching of science in primary schools had only been a legal requirement for nine years. This success represents a considerable achievement.

The development of ideas about children learning science

The development of science has influenced the overall aims of primary education. Many schools aim to enable children to gain the confidence to stimulate their curiosity, to foster their desire and abilities to learn and to develop a range of skills, interests and conceptual knowledge. Children are encouraged to develop the attitudes and foundation concepts that they can draw on in later study. These aims are very similar to those represented in earlier work: for instance, the Schools Council 'Science 5 to 13' project discussed primary science in terms of processes rather than teaching facts:

science involves exploration and exploration involves the gathering of evidence through observation, raising questions, proposing enquiries, practical investigations, finding patterns and communicating findings.

(Schools Council, 1972, pp. 5–6)

Harlen, a major contributor to the Science 5 to 13 project, emphasises the role of process skills

 The development of understanding in science is thus dependent on the ability to carry out process skills in a scientific manner. (Harlen, 1996, p. 14)

The development of process skills in primary science is important because these skills support the development of scientific concepts, which lead to scientific understanding. There seems to be broad international agreement (see Harlen, 1996; Harnqvist and Burgen, 1997; Hollins and Whitby, 1998; Peacock, 1997) that these process skills include:

 observing (collecting evidence and measurement)
hypothesising (raising questions, linking concepts)
planning (raising questions, predicting, devising enquiries)
interpreting (considering evidence, evaluating)
communicating (presenting reports, using secondary sources)

(Harlen, 1996, p. 28)

Primary science within the National Curriculum for both early years and later years sits very comfortably within this framework. Primary science is an active learning process that involves children in developing their understanding through testing their ideas against evidence. The key to primary science is involving children in structured practical activities, which lead into investigations, to find out about the world around them. These investigations involving process skills assist in the formation and understanding of scientific concepts.

Primary science is about:
■ raising questions, solving problems, exploration;
■ observation, identifying similarities and differences;
■ sorting and grouping, classifying, predicting;
■ hypothesising and devising and testing suitable activities to widen children's experience of the world and help them interact with it in a systematic and meaningful way.

Unlike historical evidence, scientific evidence is based on investigation, the formulation of hypotheses and the repetition of investigations to test the hypotheses. Encouraging primary children to investigate allows them to work like scientists, to experience unfamiliar situations and to use these experiences to develop scientific concepts. Learning science and doing science develop alongside each other.

As an example of this, the Case Study below outlines some work on the burning of materials with Years 2 and 6. With increases in central heating in homes and reduction in coal fires many children have little experience of watching materials burn. Working with two class teachers we decided that, before an investigation with controlled variables could take place, small supervised groups of children needed to see what happens to objects when they are set on fire.

Case Study 1

We used small pieces of nylon (about 6cm square), polyester, wood, metal, foam, and so on. These were each placed on a flame resistant board and set on fire (in the playground with proper safety considerations). The sheer excitement of this activity meant the first observations by the children were not as detailed as the teacher hoped. But now the children had some ideas of what to expect, and the safety implications, so they could try the activity themselves. They repeated the investigation, observing all safety procedures, noticing soot formation, speed of burning, flames, heat, smoke, smell and fumes. They also focused on using and applying science skills. The discussion that followed this activity clarified the children's ideas about burning and reactions that took place. The older children were introduced to and developed the concept of chemical reactions as a particular form of reaction. Younger children learned that materials are different and can change.

These observations were then related to their personal situation: to toys, clothes and their houses. This interlinking of science and the real world led the children to explore values with questions like 'Why do toy manufacturers not use the safest materials?' The Year 6 class followed up this experience with a life skills day run by the emergency services. One activity with the fire brigade had groups of children in a special caravan. A fire was simulated with artificial smoke and the children's escape timed. They discovered that they would all have died in a real fire. Clear links were made between the materials burnt in science and those in the caravan.

As teachers, our aim is to find suitable experiences matched to the cognitive ability of the children but also experiences that will challenge and support the children's formation of scientific concepts.

The Case Study above illustrates the way in which children can investigate the same phenomena at different ages. For example, a 3-year-old playing with cars may find out that two things rolling down a slope don't always get to the bottom at the same time. This may represent a real achievement. A 5-year-old may find some cars run down a slope quicker than others or one car may roll further than the other on reaching the bottom. The child's interpretation may be that the red or yellow car is best because it goes the furthest. For the 7-year-olds some type of measurement, for example, distance rolled and time taken, would be expected. In Year 6 it would be reasonable to expect a clearly formed hypothesis, accurate measurement, repetition of the enquiry, averaging of results and a clear statement as to whether the evidence supports the hypothesis. For a good GCSE candidate the same activity can be explained in terms of 'g' – the acceleration due to gravity. It is not the activities that are so important but what we do with them. Simply investigating or exploring the world is not really science. For children to behave scientifically their teachers must support them in applying scientific processes.

When we plan for and teach science we need to use our own knowledge and skills to move the children's understanding on. The psychologist Vygotsky (in Wood, 1988) talks about children building on their experience and knowledge and, with the help of their teachers and others, gaining new knowledge and skills. The teacher's role is to 'scaffold' the pupil's understanding from what they know to new knowledge. Ideas are explored and from that exploration new meanings should be constructed leading to understanding of science concepts. This understanding has to be appropriate to the age of the child and their level of learning. The child is encouraged to interact with science knowledge, provided by the teacher or through books, video, and computer programs. The child's existing knowledge supports the construction of new meanings. This learning process is referred to as the *constructivist theory of learning*.

A range of research into the teaching and learning of primary science based on this model started in the 1970s and continued during the 1980s and 1990s. Research by Harlen (1977, 1985, 1996), Driver et al. (1985), Osborne and Freyberg (1985), Black (1993), Hollins and Whitby (1998) and others presented the view that children construct scientific meaning through mental images and thus the constructivist view of teaching emerged. Pollard (1990) and others suggest how this meaning is socially constructed. Children, according to the constructivist model, do not start an activity with an empty mind, they bring their own ideas.

This model suggests that primary teachers need a sound understanding of science so that they can plan structured activities for children, understand where they are leading the children and know how to respond to individual children's learning. The constructivist teacher will present the same science in different ways that may make sense to different children. They will also challenge some 'common sense' views with scientific ideas.

Pollard (1990) suggests children should be

 . . . helped across the zone of proximal development, that extension of their understanding or skill that they can reach if appropriately supported.

(Pollard, 1990, p. 60)

The 'good' teacher of primary science uses their own knowledge to interpret and adapt science to various contexts and teaching situations. The teacher's flexible use of science knowledge is particularly important in early years.

 Science is a major area of human mental and practical activity which generates knowledge, knowledge that can be the basis of important technological applications as well as of intellectual satisfaction. It is an important part of education for all not just scientists to be aware of the status and nature of scientific knowledge, how it is created and how dependable it is.

(Harlen, 1996, p. 2)

Teaching science to primary school age children is about providing experiences and helping children to structure those experiences. Sometimes children will need guidelines, direction or even detailed explanations. Sometimes they will be able to explore and investigate to find out for themselves. However, what the child understands from the teacher's explanation will vary with the practical experiences you, the teacher, have given.

There is more to science than just the National Curriculum. School trips and residential visits, classroom visitors, exciting and fun activities can all enrich the classroom 'science' experience for children. Topical science from the media can also stimulate science issues beyond the National Curriculum programmes of study but be equally worthy of study. Casual observations or events in children's lives can be the stimulus for exciting scientific learning. An example is outlined in the Case Study below.

Case Study 2

A class of children, their teacher and a supporting advisory teacher, were learning about colour and light. A Year 2 (infant) class were covering colour and light and discussing the colours of a rainbow. A child mentioned that you got rainbows on the road. After some discussion it emerged the child had seen rainbow colours in puddles of water which were polluted with oil. Not all the children were aware of this factor. The class teacher arranged that they would spend an afternoon exploring puddles and water in the playground later in the term. Letters were sent home to parents. Extra helpers were sought and the children spent time making lists of things to find out and investigate. On the day the children wore old clothes, wellington boots and waterproof coats. They brought a range of paddling pools and containers for the playground. Parents assembled these.

A hose pipe was used to fill pools and buckets and wet the playground. The children made rainbow puddles, used water as mirrors, coloured the water with dyes and paint, looked at how different materials, clothes, paper, bricks reacted to water, explored refraction, water droplets and so on. This took place in small groups with children moving in groups from one activity to another, each activity being led by an adult.

The children enjoyed the afternoon and thought they were not really doing any work. What to them seemed like a succession of fun activities were in fact carefully planned and structured by the class teacher and advisory teacher.

Returning to the classroom the teacher planned that recording would be done mostly by labelled drawings. She chose this method, so that the writing of language would not get in the way of scientific thinking and understanding.

As a class the children discussed what they had seen, done and found out. They had many exciting things to tell. Prompts and prepared word lists on pieces of card were placed on each table. From this recall and drawing task the children began raising questions and asked to redo some of the tasks.

The second afternoon was a mixture of repeating some activities, observing carefully and drawing and labelling. Some children raised problems such as the pencil and wax crayons they had did not match the same shades as some of the dyed water.

Further observational drawing followed on the third afternoon and groups of children were led into developing a specific investigation that looked at making the test fair and prepared exact instructions for another group to repeat the test. The adults used questions to guide the children, questions such as: did you use 5ml, 10ml, 20ml of oil in a syringe? What sort of container was best, a wide shallow one or a tall narrow one? Did we all need to use the same amount of water? Some of these questions such as the one about syringes were closed specific questions, others were much more open ended.

The children developed a clear but simple recording framework. This they continued to use but some groups saw the need for giving more information. The children gained confidence in learning, their curiosity was stimulated and they saw the need to record and report back to others.

Models of learning

In the section above we briefly outlined an approach based on the child's construction of scientific knowledge. Stimulus response (SR) models of learning offer an alternative. They are based on the idea that if a given behaviour produces a result, which is liked by the learner, that behaviour is likely to be repeated. The theory has been used to develop some of the learning schemes (for example, DISTAR) and behaviour modification schemes that have been used in special schools. In these schemes, outcomes, which the teacher wishes to encourage, are rewarded in some way that the pupils value (for example, tokens that can be 'cashed in' at the school shop, or be used to 'buy' the right to choose activities in some part of the day). SR theories say nothing about *how* the learning takes place; instead they concentrate on the observed outcomes and how these can be achieved. In these broad terms there is nothing very startling about the theory and, apparently, little beyond the obvious that they can offer you as you plan your teaching. However, a slightly closer look changes that.

One key idea is that the reward has to be something the *pupil* values, not something the teacher thinks the pupil ought to value. Praise for a right answer in class might seem to you like a suitable reward, and for some pupils it would indeed fulfil that function. But for others, keen to enhance their status in a peer group that is not well disposed to learning, or to those who are shy, it could be the very last thing they want. Such praise would therefore fail to achieve the result that you intended, and may indeed be entirely counterproductive.

Another significant insight is that the rewards for desired outcomes are more powerful than punishment for undesired outcomes. Thus SR presents a more predictable outcome than punishment which may powerfully reinforce undesired outcomes such as science is unpleasant. This leads to such ideas as the importance of 'catching them being good', that is, of the teacher noticing and in a way that is positive for the pupil, acknowledging moments of good learning or good behaviour, rather than giving extended attention to misbehaviour. This is not a totally unexpected insight, so it is perhaps surprising that we hear pupils reporting that their teachers tend to talk to them only about things which are bad in their work (Haggarty, Hines and Postlethwaite, in press). Of course, this may not have been the reality of the situation: teachers may have been saying much that was positive. But it was the pupils' perception of the situation and as such is likely to be a powerful influence on their subsequent learning or behaviour. You may be tempted to justify concentration on unsatisfactory aspects of learning on the grounds that comments on what is in need of improvement are necessary in order to bring about that improvement. Nevertheless SR theory may be offering us a warning that such a focus is unlikely to lead to success, and underpins more recent advice such as say 'three positive things for every negative thing . . .'

SR theory also suggests that, to influence a pupil's behaviour in a particular way, we should begin by rewarding responses which are broadly acceptable, then gradually focus in on the precise response which we are seeking, ultimately reserving the reward for responses of precisely the kind we want. The theory suggests that learning within the SR framework should involve repetition of the opportunity to respond and of reward when the right response is provided, and that rewards should be contingent on the production of the desired behaviour (i.e. that rewards should be provided within the session in which the activities are taking place). It also suggests that the most effective reward regimes are those in which the pupil is rewarded at a fixed rate (for example one reward for every three correct responses in the session) but that the actual timing of the rewards is varied so that the pupil may go for several correct responses without getting a reward and then get rewards every time for the next two or three correct responses. If this seems odd, the addictive nature of computer games in which the reward strategy is often of this kind, is perhaps useful supportive evidence!

SR approaches to teaching are of proven value in supporting individuals with significant learning problems and in helping to improve unacceptable behaviour. Though they do not match well with all of our aims as science teachers, they may be especially relevant when we are planning ways to help pupils learn specific practical skills such as the use of a thermometer, or measuring instrument. As suggested above, they also help us to rethink things that we do as a matter of course (for example, to ensure that our rewards really are things that our pupils value). Also, as we shall see later, they are valuable in supporting the learning of discriminations. They are certainly one useful tool in our armoury.

Another useful theory is that of Ausubel (1968) who contrasted rote learning with meaningful learning and stressed that to encourage the latter we need to help pupils link new ideas to their existing ideas, modifying those existing ideas if necessary in order to do so. One way of doing this is to provide pupils with Advance Organisers (AOs) at the start of a piece of teaching. These are essentially bridges between what the pupils already know and what we wish to teach them. They identify the relevant bits of existing knowledge and, in broad conceptual terms, they outline what is to be covered in the lesson, working at a rather more abstract level than will be the case in the main part of that lesson. The nature of an AO gives us quite useful guidance, enabling us to make the introductory five minutes as powerful as possible.

There are, however, two additional points to make in this very brief outline of some of Ausubel's ideas. First, he draws attention to the fact that where pupils' existing ideas are in need of change, it can be very difficult to bring about that change. We will have more to say about this point when we come to look at constructivist theories of learning.

Secondly, others have shown (Cronbach and Snow, 1981) that although AOs do indeed improve the outcomes achieved by many learners; they can depress the achievements of the most able pupils. The reasons for this are not clear. Maybe, in designing the AO, we misjudge the starting point for the able learners so the 'bridge' misses the bank of the river at one end! Maybe the able pupils are switched on to the broad conceptual terms with which the AO deals and then fail to engage with the more concrete or specific content of the lesson – consequently doing less well in tests based on that content. This suggests that one justifiable way in which we could differentiate science teaching would be to provide AOs for most sets, but not for the top set; or in a mixed ability class to provide AOs in written form on most worksheets but omit them from the worksheets for the most able. Of course, it might also suggest that the planned lesson was simply inappropriate for the able pupils in that they really needed to work at the higher level indicated by the AO itself.

Ausubel provides us with the oft quoted and very powerful message that we should design our teaching to start from where the pupil is. This suggests that we really need a clear understanding of how ideas are linked in logical sequences. With such an understanding, if pupils are at A and we want to get to D, we can effectively analyse the intermediate steps that we need to tackle. Similarly if we find some pupils having difficulty with a piece of learning, which we thought should be possible for them, we can analyse more clearly what the precursors of that learning are and therefore begin to explore what might be missing in the prior learning of those individuals.

One useful source of insight is Gagné's (1974) work on hierarchies. Briefly summarised this theory emphasises that problem solving in the intellectual domain relies on rules which themselves require an understanding of concepts that in turn make use of discriminations that are themselves based on more fundamental intellectual skills, which are usually established before schooling begins. This has several consequences.

When pupils have difficulties with learning we may well think to ask whether they have a firm and appropriate grasp of relevant concepts, but how often do we go back further and ask if they can make the appropriate discriminations? Imagine a pupil facing a lesson on sound. You may be trying to establish the rule that when long objects vibrate they produce low notes whereas short objects produce high notes. If a pupil is having difficulty with this rule you might think to check that they have the concepts of pitch and of length, but it would be easy to overlook the possibility that they may not be discriminating between high and low notes effectively. Interestingly Gagné's advice on how to teach discriminations is very close to that set out earlier in this chapter when we discussed SR theories. A strategy based on an SR approach could be built into a game (where, for example, correct discriminations would allow the pupil to move further round the board) or into a computer-based learning task.

Gagné divides concepts into concrete and defined concepts. Concrete concepts can be identified by direct observation – thus 'girl' would be a concrete concept. Defined concepts are more abstract and require information beyond observation – thus 'sister' would be a defined concept. Some things can be appreciated on both levels. Thus one pupil might describe something as a circle because she has the concrete concept of a circular shape and can recognise examples which fit; another may view 'circle' as a defined concept and therefore appreciate that all points on a circle are the same distance from the centre. The second of these pupils would cope well with a lesson in which the teacher is using the circular shape of waves from a stone falling into water to show that water waves move at the same speed in all directions. The first pupil would have no basis for this understanding. Gagné's analysis therefore alerts us to possible explanations of situations which otherwise might seem quite bizarre. Two pupils with apparently the same prior knowledge (that the shape of the wave is a circle) nevertheless differ vastly in their ability to comprehend the lesson about speed.

In discussing the learning of concrete concepts, Gagné argues that pupils must be able to make the appropriate discriminations and the teacher must ensure that they are given lots of examples of the concept, *and lots of non-examples.* By providing lots of examples we can ensure that the pupil's view of the concept is sufficiently wide (for example, that they recognise that spiders and worms, as well as dogs and cats, are animals). By providing non-examples we can ensure that their view is appropriately bounded (for example that they recognise that stirring is outside the boundaries of the concept 'convection' even though there are some points in common between the two).

Defined concepts make bigger demands on the pupils. An example might be 'current is a flow of charge'. To understand this concept pupils must have an accurate understanding of the concepts of charge and of flow. If their understanding of charge does not include positive and negative they will have difficulty with current flow in liquids. If their idea of flow is of a one-way process, they will have difficulty with alternating current. There is, therefore, much more to the teaching of a defined concept than persuading the pupils to parrot back the string of words that make up the definition. The exciting thing is that finding ways to provide a suitably rich understanding of such concepts is such a fascinating aspect of teaching science.

At the top of Gagné's hierarchy lie rules. Pupils use rules when they infer the acidity of a liquid from a litmus test; they use rules when they classify a cell under a microscope as an animal cell or a plant cell; they use rules when they calculate an unbalanced force from F=ma. Clearly, defined concepts are one kind of rule, so the insights into teaching rules encompass those points made above. But Gagné also argues that the teaching of rules should ensure that:
- pupils are told what the rule will enable them to do;
- pupils are helped to review the concepts involved in the rule;
- having learnt the rule they are asked to show that they can use it as well as state it.

The final theory, which we have already discussed very briefly in this chapter, is constructivism. The basic idea here is that pupils make sense of their world by setting up for themselves (constructing) personal explanations of phenomena that work for them most of the time. For example, from their experience, pupils may argue that wood floats 'because it's wood'. This 'construct' seems to work pretty well in the situations they meet in everyday life, so the teacher's insistence on other (and actually more demanding) explanations of floating and sinking, is met with surprise. This makes pupils' constructs remarkably persistent – echoing Ausubel's point that it is hard to change a pupil's pre-existing knowledge when that is necessary in order to accommodate new knowledge.

This is a very interesting notion. It suggests that pupils are behaving very much in the ways in which we would like to see them behave as scientists – observing their environment, creatively developing rules and testing them against subsequent experience. However, because their observations are of a limited range of cases, or are in some way faulty, the rules they create are not in line with the formal scientific rules that we want them to acquire. In our work with pupils it is therefore vital that we respect and encourage the process in which they are engaging while persuading them to accept that there are problems with the models they have constructed and offering them more powerful models to use in future. This leads to the view that we should find out what constructs pupils have, should offer evidence that does not fit with these constructs, and should then show that the formal scientific ideas can cope with this troublesome evidence as well as with the evidence that they have met in the past.

For example, we find out that pupils think wood floats because it's wood; we show them that a dense hardwood sinks in alcohol; we develop the normal rules of floating and sinking; we show that these work in the everyday situations where their idea worked; we show them that the formal scientific ideas work in the new situation where their idea did not work; we argue that the scientific explanation is more powerful than theirs. However, we emphasise that their problem arose simply because of their limited experience. (They don't get to float wood on alcohol very often!)

This is a powerful way of working, which is beginning to influence not only other subject areas of the formal curriculum, but also workers in fields such as genetic counselling where lay understanding of genetics can make the counsellor's task of providing explanations of genetic diseases extremely difficult. It is therefore worth a little more attention.

How can we find out what pupils' pre-existing constructs are? One approach is to look at the research literature to see what pupils in general think about the specific issues in which we are interested (see for example Driver et al., 1985, which provides a good summary of findings across the range of science topics). Another is to understand the general characteristics of pupils' ideas so that we are able to predict what they might think in a given case. So, for example, it is useful to know that pupils tend to think of change as a one-way process and therefore have difficulties with ideas such as chemical equilibrium, which rely on appreciation of two-way processes. However, the only reliable way to access the constructs of your pupils is to elicit them from your pupils. This can be done through a brainstorming session with the group, drawing mind or concept maps, through written tasks (particularly novel ones such as 'You are a water molecule in a block of ice. Describe your experiences as the ice melts'), or through one to one interviews with pupils.

Finally, what more can we do to support pupils in changing their constructs? Presenting evidence that doesn't fit their model (a so-called cognitive conflict) is a crucial step. It opens the way to learning. However, it is unrealistic to expect pupils to create the scientific explanation for themselves given this new piece of evidence. (After all it took some of the best scientists years through the centuries to do so.) Therefore direct teaching using all the possible techniques of teacher talk, practical work, videos, computer simulations, group work, text-based learning and so forth will be necessary. But the cognitive conflict and the subsequent teaching will not be enough. We are asking pupils to put forward their personal ideas and we are challenging those ideas and expecting change. This is only likely to happen if the pupils feel valued and supported even if their ideas are shown to be incomplete. Perhaps, for the teacher, the most demanding element in constructivist teaching is the need to create a supportive classroom environment in which no idea is ridiculed either by teacher or other pupils, and in which the basic value of the pupil's process of construction is celebrated even when the results of that process are in need of change.

The science challenge for the future

Today's science is too complex and ever changing for the curriculum to be restricted to a body of given knowledge. Primary science has focused on processes partly as a response to the dynamic nature of the subject. The writers of the Advanced Oxford Dictionary (1998) estimate that the English language, including Australian and American, is growing at a net rate of 8000 words a year. Of those new words 60 per cent are scientific or technological. Thus in computers, in science, in communications such as air traffic control, English has become the dominant international language. The society in which we and our children live is based on science and technology. The homes in which we live are full of scientific and technological applications. The teaching of science needs to enable children to make sense of the world through knowing factual information and extending that to understanding through practical science, hands-on activities.

❝ *Pupils should develop an understanding that science is a human activity, that scientific ideas change through time, and that the nature of scientific ideas*

and the uses to which they are put are affected by the social and cultural con-
texts in which they are developed.   (DES, 1988, p. 70 Attainment Target 22)

Of course factual information from a range of book and computer material is important in supporting learning but learning science is not simply the rote learning of facts. Learning science is learning an attitude, a way of investigating and thinking about the world.

Any explanation given to a child in response to the inevitable 'why?' must be relevant to that child. Finding responses to questions that are appropriate to particular children is not easy and comes largely from experience. Learning should be fun as well as being challenging. It should be fun and enjoyable for the teacher as well.

Enquiry task 2

Reflect on some of your most memorable learning experiences.
Were these recent or old experiences?
Was the learning simple or complex?
Was the learning enjoyable or not?
Why have you remembered them?
What was significant about these experiences to you?

Write down two of these learning experiences.
Try and analyse what was important about these experiences to you. Write down your reflective views on each experience.

Enquiry task 3

Reflect on some science learning that you have done at school, in training, whilst teaching, through watching television, through gardening, through house repairs.

Select one area of science learning you remember in detail.
What made this science learning significant?
Was it the context, the knowledge, the effort put in, or something else?
Write down your analysis and compare this to the learning experiences in Enquiry task 2.

Children in Britain today live in a complex technological society. Remote controls for television, mobile phones and flushing toilets are standard features of our lives. Good science teaching should enable children to understand and to find answers to questions about how these things work such as: how does sound travel to mobile phones or why does water go down pipes and not up? Such questions include technology and the application of science in explaining how various appliances work. Some questions may concern the society in which we live and influence the decisions we make in our lives. Involvement with such questions may help to make modern science ideas accessible to children.

The intention today remains similar to that of Josiah Mason in 1872, that all children are taught science in primary schools to a satisfactory standard. The focus at the start of the twenty-first century is on developing an integration between science knowledge and skills so that children can construct meaning and conceptual understandings. The teacher may structure the practical work to guide the children, or develop more open investigations which allow them to try their own ideas. Some of these scientific experiences will be directed at enabling children to see that many common sense interpretations of the world around them do not match formal scientific concepts. In this way, through their school science experiences, children's understanding of formal scientific concepts are extended and developed.

With advances in medical technology it is estimated that many infant children today will live healthy lives beyond a 100-years-old. These children may see the twenty-second century. We should prepare children as well as we can in science to make sense of the world and its phenomena as we know it and to be able to respond to the many changes that will take place.

 Do we want all our future citizens to understand and speak the language of science? In other words, do we want a population accepting that it is good for everyone to be scientific in the way they deal with problems in everyday life or are we happy to go on thinking that there are a few clever people who become scientists, while most of us never will? (Peacock, 1997, p. 12)

Note

1   See for example; the Royal Society of Chemistry; the Institutes of Biology and Physics; the Oxford University Primary School Teachers and Science Project (PSTS, 1993); the Liverpool University Science Process and Concept Exploration Project (Space, 1990–1998); the Assessment of Performance Units (APU, 1990) research findings in science and the Schools Council Project '*Science 5 to 13*' (1973)

References

ASSESSMENT OF PERFORMANCE UNIT (1983) *Science at Age 11*, London: APU/DES.

ASSOCIATION FOR SCIENCE EDUCATION (1994) *Be Safe*, London: ASE.

AUSUBEL, D. P. (1968) *Educational Psychology: A Cognitive View*, New York: Holt Rinehart and Winston.

BLACK, P. and LUCAS, M. (eds) (1993) *Children's Informal Ideas in Science*, London: Routledge.

BURGES, D. (1997) *Times Educational Supplement*, May 1997.

CRONBACH, L. J. and SNOW, R. E. (1981) *Aptitudes and Instructional Methods: Handbook for Research of Interactions*, New York: Irvington.

DES (1985) *Science 5 to 16: A Statement of Policy*, London: HMSO.

DES (1988) *Science for Ages 5 to 16*, London: HMSO.

DES (1989) *Science in the National Curriculum*, London: HMSO.

DES (1991) *Science in the National Curriculum*, London: HMSO.

DFE (1995) *Key Stages 1 and 2 of the National Curriculum*, London: HMSO.

DRIVER, R., GUESNE, E. and TIBERGHEIN, D. (1985a) *Children's Ideas in Science*, Milton Keynes: OUP.

FARROW, S. (1996) *The Really Useful Science Book*, London: Falmer Press.

GAGNÉ, R. M. and BRIGGS, L. J. (1974) *Principles of Instructional Design*, New York: Holt, Rinehart and Winston.

GAGNÉ, R. (1977) *The Conditions of Learning: Learning Methods*, New York: Holt, Rinehart and Winston.

HAGGERTY, HINES and POSTLETHWAITE (in press).

HARLEN, W. (1977) *Match and Mismatch: Finding Answers*, London: Oliver and Boyd.

HARLEN, W. (1977) *Match and Mismatch: Raising Questions*, London: Oliver and Boyd.

HARLEN, W. (1985) *Primary Science: Taking the Plunge*, London: Heinemann.

HARLEN, W. (1996) *The Teaching of Science in Primary Schools*, London: David Fulton.

HARNQVIST, K. and BURGEN, A. (1997) *Growing up with Science. Developing Early Understanding of Science*, Bristol: Jessica Kingsley.

HIBBERT, C. (1975) *The Illustrated London News: Social History of Victorian Britain*, London: BCA.

HOLLINS, M. and WHITBY, V. (1998) *Progression in Primary Science. A Guide to the Nature and Practice of Science in Key Stages 1 and 2*, London: David Fulton.

HMI (1978) *Primary Education in England: A Survey by HM Inspectors of Schools, 1978*, London: HMSO.

HMI (1983 to 1987) *Curriculum Matters from 5 to 16 Series*, Department of Education and Science, London: HMSO.

NCC (1989) *Science in the National Curriculum*, London: DES.

OFSTED (1998) *Standards in Primary Science*, London: OFSTED Publications.

OSBORNE, R. and FREYBERG, P. (1985) *Learning in Science. The Implications of Children's Science*, Auckland: Heinemann.

PEACOCK, A. (1997) *Opportunities for Science in the Primary School*, Staffordshire: Trentham Books.

POLLARD, A. (1990) *Learning in Primary Schools*, London: Cassell Education.

QUALIFICATIONS AND ASSESSMENT AUTHORITY AND DfEE (1998) *Science: A Scheme of Work for Key Stages 1 and 2*, London: QCA.

RICHARDS, C. and HOLFORD, D. (eds) (1983) *The Teaching of Primary Science: Policy and Practice*, London: Falmer Press.

SCIENCE 5 TO 13 (1972) *With Objectives in Mind*, London: Macdonald Educational.

UNIVERSITY OF LIVERPOOL (1990–1998) *Primary Science Processes and Concept Exploration (SPACE) Project*, Liverpool: Liverpool University Press.

UNIVERSITY OF OXFORD, WESTMINSTER COLLEGE (1993) *Understanding Science Concepts, Primary Teachers and Science (PSTS) Project*, Oxford: OUP.

WOOD, D. (1988) *How Children Think and Learn*, Oxford: Basil Blackwell.

Chapter 9

The nature and purpose of primary science

Kate Ashcroft, Gordon Guest and Keith Postlethwaite

Purposes in science

Whether or not children are taught science they will develop their own ideas and understanding of science. In many cases these untutored views will be incorrect, creating misconceptions for the individual. Practical experiences in science can teach children how to identify good science questions, enable them to extend and enrich their learning and existing knowledge, and help them construct concepts from their experience.

Within this section we shall explore the perceived purposes of science and how these purposes support and enable learning in science. The context for exploring these issues will be drawn from a number of experiences with children who visited Paignton Zoo for a week-long residential trip. These experiences took place over several years with different classes of junior children. In many schools residential trips or school camps are a routine feature of the school year. These particular residential trips aimed to develop the children's understanding of the variety of life in science through studying many animals in the zoo at first hand and to extend their knowledge through secondary sources in school. The children used this information to write a project book. The idea was to help the children make sense of the world in which they live and to see the relevance of scientific explanations. The zoo visit enabled children to combine images from television, video and books with real life observations.

Science and its technological products, space ships, telephones, as well as environmental and health issues, such as drugs, fitness, pollution, and ecological changes have an impact on people's personal lives. Global warming and chemically engineered food crops are topical issues. In both cases non-scientists support a particular argument with scientific evidence. Peacock (1997) argues that these wider issues of science have been eroded during the various science curriculum rewrites in the English Science National Curriculum. In placing 'variations of living things' from the National Curriculum in a context of animal habitats, the scientific learning for children was placed in a familiar context: that of keeping animals. The science learning in terms of classification and animal habitat were the central themes but other learning, such as co-operation and independence also occurred. We wanted to develop an understanding of science as it related to the children's lives and a range of social issues. The aim was to develop scientifically literate children, able to make informed choices about the science and technology they live with now and in the future.

In the zoo visit, the planned science involved process skills and acquiring new knowledge. This new knowledge varied from information, such as when you stroke a snake you do so in one direction because of its scales, to refining ideas they already had. For instance they knew a rhinoceros was big but did not expect it to be as big as it was – as Lucy commented, 'It's as big as my dad's car'. In looking at variations of living things, pupils learnt how to sort and classify different species: for example they learnt that there are different species and families and that there are non-scientific and scientific ways to sort animals. In learning to classify these living things the children realised that a zoo holds a small fraction of the variety of living species in the world.

Through developing the ideas of 'variations of living things' the children were involved in using scientific process skills, observation, finding evidence, interpreting that evidence and explanation. The visit to the zoo provided access to first hand experiences, sounds, smells and size that were not available from books, video or CD ROM in the same way. The children interpreted that evidence, through questioning and comparing it with what they already knew. Initially the children were learning through the constructivist model, constructing their own understanding on the evidence of their senses. However through peer and teacher discussion their learning was 'scaffolded'.

Science involves children in developing an ability to investigate and interpret the information obtained. In this way children construct meaning to enhance the understanding of concepts. Thus primary science is part of a broader curriculum that contributes to the general intellectual, personal and social growth of pupils. Primary science education is not an isolated experience, concerned solely with developing scientific knowledge. The children used the linked experiences of studying the variety of life and a visit to the zoo to develop logical explanations, present arguments and reach conclusions not just about the variety of life, but the role of zoos, of wildlife and how mankind changes habitats. They engaged with interpreting science and determining scientific values. The visit enabled the children to raise many environmental questions, such as: why did people poach rhino? what do you do if people need to farm the land the wild animals need? Specific questions concerning the size of the cheetah cage and whether to feed snakes live or dead food were also raised.

Children's misconceptions in science seem to come from their attempts to deal with incompatible pieces of information, some coming from school, some coming from within the social culture, television, video and so on and some from personal experiences or lack of personal experiences. So, for example, the children recognised all the zoo creatures as animals but the idea that people are also animals was difficult for some children to accept.

Children from rural areas who owned pets had many experiences of live animals to support what they learnt in school, whilst children with no pets from inner urban areas may not have the same experiences of live animals. Consequently, some of the children from urban areas thought that nothing happens without a human cause. Misconceptions can result from children organising limited amounts of knowledge. As their knowledge increased these children were able to interrelate more features about animals.

How do these purposes fit with models of learning?

We have already discussed the constructivist approach as a learning model favoured in science. Learning requires the child to construct mental meanings. Learning relates to outcomes and the children's prior knowledge and is a continuous and active process within and without schools. Meanings are constructed or rejected and learners have the final responsibility for what they learn.

Science as a subject is sometimes considered as value free. Take the example of electricity: electrical current enables appliances to work, it can be used in various ways and can be switched on or off. It can be generated in several ways. This is factual scientific information – domain specific – information. On the other hand, the environmental and cultural influences on science must be recognised. The body of knowledge presented in the National

Curriculum is domain specific knowledge. However the choice of whether electricity is generated by nuclear power or solar cells, are political and economic decisions that have a range of consequences. These decisions are value laden and involve situational learning. In asking pupils to relate scientific knowledge to everyday experiences we are expecting them to integrate domain specific and situational knowledge. It can be argued that the selection of knowledge and skills for inclusion within the curriculum represents itself a particular set of values. Thus a political and social view influences the science curriculum. It is important that:

 scientifically literate students can engage intelligently in public discourse and debate about matters of scientific and technological concern. (Tuomi, 1997)

To learn science pupils not only have to assimilate new concepts but also develop, modify and change existing concepts. If these concepts are to change the learner must also be willing to adapt societal views and values, which may not always be a smooth process. The implications are that learners should be encouraged to be active in their interpretations, but that they are also guided by the teacher, so that their existing knowledge base is developed or reorganised in the light of new scientific information. Emerging ideas are bigger than previous ones as they link new and older experiences together. The role for the teacher in this process is to know and understand sufficient science to guide the children and to possess the skills in a range of methods to help children make sense of scientific information.

Supporting learning in primary science

Stephen Hawking (Filkin, 1997) in his theories of cosmology and the formation of the earth, demonstrates that science involves creating new knowledge. Scientists attain this new knowledge through the use of scientific processes. Although there are many varieties of scientist and scientific work today, scientists share common views on the need and importance of producing results that can be repeated and reproduced by others. In this chapter we set out to review a range of views on what constitutes these science process skills. We illustrate this with examples of children's work on electricity and ask you to consider the links between children's process skills and the work illustrated.

Within primary science children construct scientific concepts, they build knowledge about a concept and about the way science is learnt through using the processes of science. The National Curriculum is extremely clear that science is about first hand experiences where children carry out practical activities and investigations, and in this way construct new knowledge for themselves.

Within an investigation children may be encouraged to ask questions and make predictions, plan tests, make tests fair, carry out experiments, interpret and communicate their findings. An investigation may start from a variety of different stimuli such as teacher-led discussion, pupil discussion, observation, curriculum work, television or visits. The teacher may believe that learning which builds upon the child's own thinking may provide a more secure foundation from which their understanding can be developed. In the learning process the teacher may engage in dialogue with the children so the child's ideas are given value.

There is now a growing consensus on the range of process skills involved in primary science. (See for example, Ritchie and Ollerenshaw (1997), Carre and Ovens (1994), The Association for Science Education (1993) and Harlen (1996).) Process skills are seen as central to the formation of science concepts. Hollins and Whitby (1998) suggest that process skills revolve around planning, doing and interpreting.

- *planning*, *including formulating questions from significant observation, making predictions and hypotheses which can be tested, planning fair tests in which variables are controlled;*
- *doing*, *including selecting and using equipment, observing and measuring to collect evidence, recording data;*
- *interpreting*, *including organising and presenting results, concluding with respect to predictions or hypotheses, evaluating experimental work and findings, communicating to others.* (Hollins and Whitby, 1998, p. 8)

Smith and Peacock (1995) suggest eight characteristics that make up an investigation. You might use these characteristics to map onto your teaching plans the specific skills or characteristics matched to a child's learning development, taking into account child's age, maturity and previous experience.

- *Investigations have a purpose – to find out the answer to a specific question.*
- *The investigation will turn the question into a test, which they can carry out.*
- *The test is planned so one thing is changed to see the effect(s) it produces.*
- *Other things, which might affect the results, are kept the same to make the test fair.*

- *The effects are carefully observed and if possible, measured.*
- *The observations or measurements are recorded.*
- *The results are used to shed light on the original question.*
- *The investigation might then be repeated or improved.*

(Smith and Peacock, 1995)

The development of these skills may be grouped into four broad stages.

Stage 1 developing basic skills such as:
- selecting and using equipment;
- display skills – drawing graphs;
- techniques – measuring temperature.

Stage 2 making significant observations such as:
- sorting and classification;
- seeking similarities and differences;
- provide opportunities to use knowledge and understanding, apply it to what they experience;
- be starting points for investigations by encouraging pupils to ask questions and make predictions arising from their observations.

Stage 3 undertaking illustrative (practical) work:
- this often has instructions which tell pupils what to do, what apparatus to use, what to measure, how many measurements to take and how to tabulate results;
- the purpose is to illustrate a concept or process so that pupils gain first-hand experience before discussion.

(Many children do practical science activities yet do not fully engage with the investigative process, stopping at stage 3.)

Stage 4 doing investigative work:
- investigations can stem from pupils' statements, pupils' observations, or from discussion with the teacher;
- there will be a question to test; (This will involve identifying variables, measuring and displaying the results.)
- the eight characteristics (Smith and Peacock op. cit.) will apply;
- allows pupils to select the most appropriate instruments and apparatus for an activity;
- allows a variety of routes to a solution;
- enables pupils to refine concepts from their starting points;
- investigations help pupils clarify or challenge ideas and experiences they have met or been taught.

As a reflective teacher the challenge is to ensure that children develop a range of these skills and processes.

Enquiry task 1

Look at the examples of children working (Figures 9.1, 9.2, 9.3 and 9.4). From these try and deduce which aspects of investigations the various children were involved in.

Make a list of the processes used in investigations for Key Stage 1 and another for Key Stage 2.

Relate your list to the programmes of study for science. Are there any matches?

What assumptions did you need to make, if any, in identifying these investigational processes?

Paula aged 5 (Year 1) has drawn a simple circuit showing how she can light up the bulb in several ways, although it is not always clear where the one wire used is in the diagram. She is developing an understanding of circuits being completed for them to work.

Liam aged 6 (Year 2) has much clearer diagrams. He shows the wire to the different terminals on the battery. The bump on the positive is clearly shown. He is also able to show the bulb in different positions and represent the importance of that to the circuit. He has moved beyond Pippa's stage of development and is seeing and representing a more accurate picture of circuits and the connections.

Adam aged 8 (Year 4), the diagrams show further progression. He can draw and label all the various parts and explain what he is doing. His explanations clearly show he understands making circuits and drawing them

FIG 9.1
Drawing of a simple
circuit: Yr 1

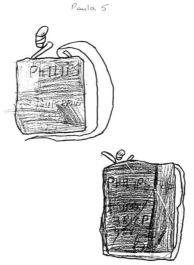

Paula 5

FIG 9.2
Circuits and connections:
Yr 2

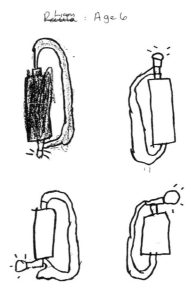

Liam : Age 6

Adam YR4

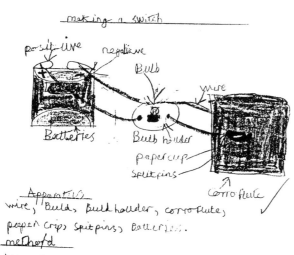

making a switch

positive   negative

Bulb

wire

Batteries   Bulb holder

paper cup

split pins

Corroflute

Apparatus
wire, Bulbs, Bulb holder, corroflute,
paper clips split pins, Batteries.

method
We cut out some corroflute and then made two holes
in the corroflute then put two split pines in the
holes and on one of the split pins we put
a paper clip. Then we joined two pieces of wire
to the split pines then one wire to the bulb holder
then the nexts wire to the Battery.

making a switch

positive   negative

wire   Buld

Buld

Batteries

Corro flute

Apparatus
wire, split pins, corro flute, Buld, Buld in a

method
We cut out some corro flute and put to two split pins
in it. Then we joined two red wires to the ends
of the split pin, then we joined one wire to a battery
another to a bulb holder then a green wire to the
battery and bulb holder.
Joel Retio. ITP

FIG 9.3
Circuits, connections and switches: showing progression: Yr 4

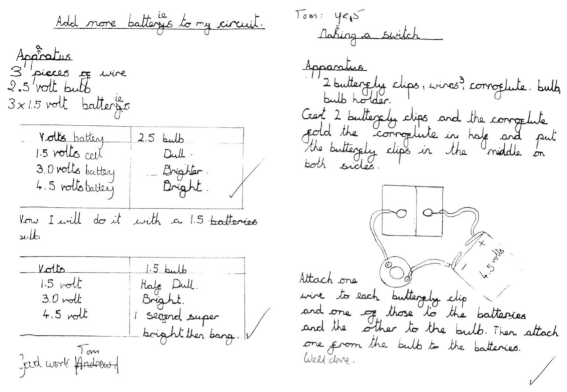

Add more batterys ie to my circuit.

Apparatus
3 pieces of wire
2.5 volt bulb
3 x 1.5 volt batterys ie

Volts battery	2.5 bulb
1.5 volts cell	Dull.
3.0 volts battery	Brighter.
4.5 volts battery	Bright.

Now I will do it with a 1.5 batteries bulb

Volts	1.5 bulb
1.5 volt	Half Dull.
3.0 volt	Bright.
4.5 volt	1 second super bright then bang.

Good work Tom Andrew

Tom: yes
Making a switch

Apparatus
2 butterfly clips, wires³, correplute. bulb, bulb holder.
Get 2 butterfly clips and the correplute fold the correplute in half and put the butterfly clips in the middle on both sides.

Attach one wire to each butterfly clip and one of those to the batteries and the other to the bulb. Then attach one from the bulb to the batteries.
Well done.

FIG 9.4
Predictions and recording results: Yr 5

using the parts and he is moving into making his own switches. He has not yet demonstrated interpreting 3-dimensional drawings into 2-dimensional symbolic representations.

Tom aged 10 (Year 5) is able to develop his investigations making predictions, setting out tables and recording the results. He has noted that he can pop a 1.5volt bulb with a 4.5volt battery. He is now demonstrating that he can use circuits for a range of investigations, which he can make fair. He can analyse results and use the results to guide his work.

We have described above a number of process skills of primary science. Can you now, as reader, identify the science skills and scientific knowledge the children's recording suggest?

Considerations for planning

In your planning for science you may find that it is helpful to have a clear idea of your learning objectives, what science the children will be doing, why they are doing the activities planned, the expected level of achievement and the consolidation activities. You might decide to use open ended investigative tasks or more structured activities. These are likely to raise different planning, organisation and management issues.

You may need to plan for the children to develop specific techniques and to understand the notion of variables. For example, when testing paper helicopters, children could be encouraged to appreciate that it might be better to test wing size and then weight rather than do both at once. The teacher needs to provide a framework or structure to support and guide the children even when they are working in an open ended manner. Children need to be supported as they learn to develop testable hypotheses and the skills of scientific investigation.

Case Study 1

Electricity with Year 2 and Year 6

Below are some of the science concepts and planning that were involved in a series of lessons on electricity with an early years class. (Year 2)

Knowledge	Skills	Understanding
know name of battery	fixing together	electricity flows
bump end	battery right way	electricity can be
flat end	using screwdriver	increased (like tap water)
wire		lights up bulb
sleeve		
bulb		
bulb holder		
light		

The terms bump end and flat end were used by the children to describe the positive and negative terminals on a cell battery. When they were ready the terms positive and negative were introduced.

With this Year 2 class the teacher developed these concepts and skills using a detailed step by step plan which included the children's open-ended tasks. She knew her children well, knew what they might wish to investigate and how to support them. Her planning included:
1   the knowledge that each activity should develop
2   the practical activities to develop this knowledge
3   the closed investigations to be suggested by the teacher (e.g. is red wire best?)
4   a focus upon some, not all, process skills
5   the open investigations the children may suggest

The teacher used the analogy of water flowing to explain electric current. She found that using analogies to relate science concepts to other experiences is not always useful. One must be alert to the fact children may then ascribe other properties which are not helpful. In using a water flow analogy to explain current the children thought that like the garden hose when there is a hole in it water leaks out, then the children may think this is the same for electricity, that it can leak out of a circuit.

When she worked with the Year 6 class on the same topic, the teacher also had clear goals but found that she needed to be flexible in responding to the pupils' varied questions and to the direction of the children's investigations. In both cases the teacher needed some background knowledge but had to be prepared for the questions she knew nothing about.

Pupils only get one chance at primary education and this needs to be well planned so that pupils get a series of experiences that progressively develop their knowledge, understanding and skills directly linked to their cognitive age and ability.

The skill of a good teacher is to take the currently accepted knowledge, understanding and skills and to interpret these for the pupils into a stimulating progression of experience that challenges pupils' current thinking and motivates them into learning based on first hand experience. Commercial schemes are published to appeal to most schools. As a reflective teacher you will wish to consider carefully whether the activities they suggest are suitable for the culture and experience of the pupils in your school.

Reflection

Look at the same topic such as magnetism in a range of schemes for example, Nuffield Primary Science, Collins Primary Science and Ginn Science and list the activities they suggest.

Would your pupils have sufficient experience to complete them with understanding? Could you use some combination of ideas or a new activity more suited to the age, ability and cultural background of the pupils in your school?

You cannot teach what you do not know, and you cannot challenge pupils' thinking appropriately if you do not know quite a bit more than pupils do. It is not part of this chapter to develop science knowledge or give examples on how to plan and carry out valid experiments. There are other books expressly written for primary teachers, for example, *Science with Reason* (Atkinson and Fleer, 1995) and *Investigations and Progression in Science* (Smith and Peacock, 1995). It is important that individual teachers understand the science curriculum sufficiently well to choose appropriate interpretations of the National Curriculum to develop the knowledge, understanding and skills of their pupils. It is pointless having a number of pupils with poor literacy skills trying to implement a curriculum that was designed for a school where literacy is above the national average.

Enquiry task 2

Design a series of science activities that require very little, if any reading.

Use exposition, video, and verbal instructions for practical work and plenty of practical exploration.

Get the pupils to feed back in pictures or diagrams, talk to you.

Get them to take a series of photographs, especially if you have a digital camera, demonstrate or give instructions to each other.

Assess the extent that the children were able to achieve scientific learning objectives.

Assess whether the omission of written language helped or hindered the achievement of those objectives.

A scheme of work should be your school's curriculum not one from another school and must be derived directly from, and referenced to, the National Curriculum. The emphasis should be on what is to be learnt and its assessment, not the activity.

Defining progression

Identifying progression is difficult, time consuming, but vital. The National Curriculum is not very helpful here and the only clear progression is that some aspects are in Key Stage 1 and others in Key Stage 2 and others in Key Stages 3 and 4. Planning needs to be more refined than this. Particularly at Key Stage 2, where there are four years to cover the curriculum, each part may need to be visited more than once and the second 'visit' should be cognitively more demanding than the first.

For example, the Science National Curriculum Key Stage 1, Science, 3, 1a says;

 Pupils should be taught; to use their senses to explore and recognise the similarities and differences between materials. (DfEE, 1995)

The idea under development here is that if two things are identical then all their properties are the same. At Key Stage 1 the properties of materials must be observable by the pupils and they should be taught the language by which they can describe them appropriately: for instance, to identify materials as hard or soft. At this stage the materials provided would need to be unambiguously hard or soft. A development would be to use a wider range of descriptions, hard, soft, flexible, stretchy, light, heavy. Next you might introduce materials that were not always clearly in a category. The final step might be to get pupils to identify similarities and differences by testing, for example, whether some objects are magnetic, others float or sink and so on. Finally, you might get pupils to draw scientific deductions for example, that not all metals are magnetic.

An activity may fulfil a range of requirements: for example, it might implement the Programmes of Study, form part of a progression of science knowledge, understanding and skills, or lead to assessment. The activity is there as a vehicle for learning. It is not an end in itself. Activities in science often involve practical work. There are various forms that serve different purposes and these need to be clear in any planning. For example there is demonstration, first hand experience to introduce or reinforce knowledge understanding and skills, and the designing of an investigation. You may focus on each separately or some combination. All are valid.

Looking at outcomes and assessment

You may find that children learn better when they are clear about the expected outcomes. A starting point may be the level descriptions of the National Curriculum. Your expectations may need to be differentiated to take account of children's abilities not just in science, but also in English and mathematics: there are many fluent readers who cannot think well in science terms and some poor writers who can. You may decide to look to the next key stage so that there are some realistic expectations of the higher achieving pupils.

The prime purpose of assessment is to assist the pupil with their learning and to identify the next appropriate steps. Assessment arrangements within the National Curriculum should not distract us from this purpose. Teachers assess continuously within the classroom. Dialogue with a pupil about learning or the work being undertaken is likely to involve assessment questions, such as:
- Does the child understand this?
- Has the pupil achieved this skill?
- What advice or question should I now offer?

Teachers gain evidence to answer these questions through activities such as focused observation, active listening, viewing the product or learning outcomes of children's work, asking the right type of question and setting appropriate and challenging tasks. In assessing pupils they need to consider the purpose of their assessment and which of the following styles of assessment is most appropriate to a particular purpose.

Formative assessment may be used by the teacher to assess a child's ongoing work. The samples of children's work discussed above indicate the stage of development of each child in their understanding of electricity. The teacher could use this evidence in his or her planning of the next stage. Failure to do this is a common weakness of formative assessment. It is clear that teachers do not always use it to inform their planning and target setting. The heart of formative assessment lies in the dialogue between teacher and learner. It is this dialogue which enables a shared understanding of the pupils' performance and understanding. Children often know what they have not done. This form of dialogue can enable them to understand what they need to do.

Summative assessment is used as evidence of a pupil's overall achievement. Examples include the annual written report to parents and the Standards Assessment Task result that shows the child has reached a particular level within the National Curriculum. Unlike formative assessment, which is about informing and mapping development, the summative assessment stands until the next summative assessment. The process is not one of dialogue but of completing a specific task in a particular way.

Diagnostic assessment is used to assist the teacher in planning particular aspects of work to help the child. The diagnosis may identify specific scientific skills, concepts or activities the child needs to aid their understanding. The teacher can then plan to teach or support those specific needs.

Personal assessment on the other hand is focused on pupils' attitudes and behaviour: for example, whether they work in a group, share equipment without arguing, or stay on task. OFSTED (1998) indicate that personal assessment is commonly used in place of formative assessment. So instead of a teacher noting that Tom (see above) understood circuits and the idea of increasing voltage, the teacher might note Tom worked well, was motivated and stayed on task. Personal assessment is important but teachers need to be aware that it differs from formative assessment in that it tends not to be focused on subject learning.

Assessment may be focused on problem solving. Such a focus enables the teacher to see how children use a range of skills and knowledge in a more open ended way. Open ended activity is very powerful as it allows children to think and work on their own whilst allowing the teacher to see if they can transfer the knowledge gained in one concept into another.

Standardised Assessment Tasks (SATs) are specific tests which children do at age 7, 11, and 14, with optional tests at age 9. Additional baseline tests are used with reception children. Such tests require specific responses that relate to specific criteria. The use of standardised criteria allows for comparisons between one child and another and one school and another in a way that is not possible with most other forms of assessment.

You could use all these forms of assessment in gathering evidence about a child and in developing their individual portfolio. You might develop assessment criteria by refining the National Curriculum level descriptions. Whatever assessment procedure is chosen it should help identify what children can do well and what they need to develop further. Assessment is there to inform and identify progress. Any summative assessment summarised as a single number defining pupils' level in terms of the National Curriculum should be referenced to and supported by a range of evidence.

Assessment raises issues of control and social justice. You might wish to consider whether when pupils are set work that is to be assessed it should be made clear to them what the criteria for the marking is going to be. You might inform them whether you would be assessing the reporting of the investigation, the science vocabulary used, whether it is written neatly, the quality of the question posed, the accuracy of measurement or some combination. Pupils particularly need to know if the assessment is related to process skills or knowledge as this may influence how they report their science. Often children do not have access to the information they need to improve, such as what do they now need to accomplish to reach the next attainment target level. As a reflective teacher you may consider that children have a right to feedback about what was done well, not so well and in particular what needs to be done to improve it.

Developing scientific knowledge with teachers

Through the preceding sections we have discussed the process skills, investigational strategies and purposes of science and illustrated these with a number of stories of classroom work. In this section we look at the question of the teaching skills needed to be an effective primary science teacher. Science is making sense of the world around us, how it works and how science connects with many technological applications in our society. With the introduction of the Teacher Training Agency Science Curriculum for Universities it seems as though this may well be a 'governmental view'.

 The purpose of primary science therefore is to equip children with the skills to tackle new situations with confidence and to develop broad conceptual knowledge and understanding as a solid base on which to develop new concepts.

(Hollins and Whitby, 1998)

However, knowing this purpose and being able to act on it as a teacher may not be that easy.

If children are to tackle new skills and concepts successfully teachers need to understand these same skills and concepts also. The National Curriculum has been helpful in defining what scientific knowledge and skills teachers need to acquire. It has also made clear that children need an understanding of some of the essential scientific ideas used by scientists. It has not addressed the question of how that is taught effectively. What is clear is that teachers of primary children need to feel confident in their content knowledge so that they may ask appropriate questions of children and provide simple spontaneous analogies to explain a difficult idea.

The Association for Science Education (ASE) in their policy paper 'Science Education for the Year 2000 and Beyond' (*Education in Science*, February 1998) indicate how science in our everyday lives, knowledge and understanding and methods of scientific enquiry interrelate. (See Figure 9.5.)

Carre and Ovens (1994) drawing on research from the Leverhulme project claim that 'those student teachers with higher levels of content knowledge and knowledge of process skills showed particular patterns of effective science teaching'. They go on to list those effective patterns as:

- *They planned in detail organisational matters and provided appropriate activities for children to make sense of science.*
- *Their presentation at the beginning of the lesson explained its purpose and offered a clear link with the practical work that followed.*
- *Their teaching approaches were flexible and included both knowledge telling and knowledge transforming methods.*
- *They were able to generate and use instructional representations.*
- *They were good listeners, respected children's prior knowledge and indicated if their responses were correct or inappropriate. They were able to challenge children's ideas and beliefs.* (Carre and Ovens, 1994)

FIG 9.5
The purposes of science education arising from consultation

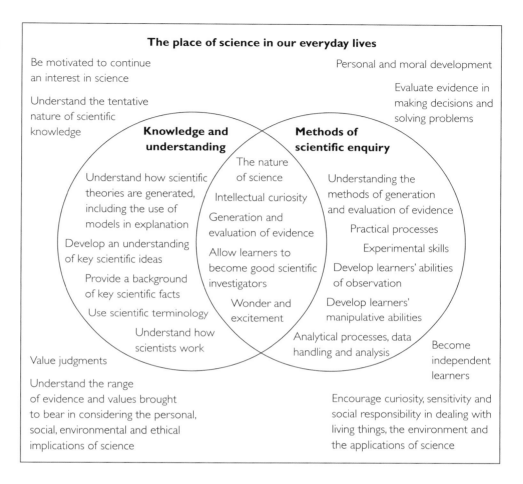

The place of science in our everyday lives

Be motivated to continue an interest in science

Personal and moral development

Evaluate evidence in making decisions and solving problems

Understand the tentative nature of scientific knowledge

Knowledge and understanding

Methods of scientific enquiry

Understand how scientific theories are generated, including the use of models in explanation

The nature of science

Intellectual curiosity

Generation and evaluation of evidence

Allow learners to become good scientific investigators

Wonder and excitement

Understanding the methods of generation and evaluation of evidence

Practical processes

Experimental skills

Develop learners' abilities of observation

Develop learners' manipulative abilities

Develop an understanding of key scientific ideas

Provide a background of key scientific facts

Use scientific terminology

Understand how scientists work

Analytical processes, data handling and analysis

Become independent learners

Value judgments

Understand the range of evidence and values brought to bear in considering the personal, social, environmental and ethical implications of science

Encourage curiosity, sensitivity and social responsibility in dealing with living things, the environment and the applications of science

---

Being able to challenge children's beliefs through having a secure scientific knowledge themselves is something many teachers, even experienced teachers, find challenging. It is useful for teachers to have a knowledge of the key concepts but they also need to understand how to teach that knowledge and how children will learn. Research projects such as the SPACE project (Liverpool University 1990–1998) have illustrated how children may understand solids and liquids but struggle with gases.

One approach to developing a teaching sequence is outlined in the Case Study below which involves discussion and extended practical work. One of the difficulties with this approach is time. Teachers may feel they cannot allow children the time they need to explore a range of concepts. The QCA scheme addresses this issue through using the spiral curriculum model. Within such a model the children have regular and repeated experience over several years. Such a model is helpful in planning but, within the classroom, teachers still need to be aware that some children may have a greater understanding and others less, that some may grasp more abstract concepts whilst others need concrete experiences.

Case Study 2

This example looks at a cohort of 140 BA (QTS) students who investigated questions concerned with earth and space. Even at university level students come with misconceptions about science or lack of awareness. In the unit 'Earth and Space' it was apparent that the majority of the students could not explain why the sun was lower in the winter and higher in the summer. Within a cohort of 140, many did not realise there was a difference. Of the 31 students who knew about these differences and could explain them 20 were science specialists.

The following teaching sequence model was used:

introductory discussion:	from this questions were raised
observation:	a range of photographs of space, torches, globes, balls and models were discussed and handled
further discussion:	The students came up with an explanation of the sun's apparent movement
practical work:	in small groups they collected their resources and explored the question
significant observation:	they began to notice significant features of the task
recording:	notes were made and tests rechecked
further discussion:	each group came together for a whole class discussion

It was quite clear students' knowledge was not scientifically based and they used everyday notions to explain scientific phenomena. The challenge the scientific explanation posed to existing knowledge domains was considerable. They were presented with a question from a Year 6 Standardised Assessment Task (SAT) paper for children aged 11 years, which many found challenging. They became motivated to find an answer. The concern was not that the SAT needed answering rather that this was considered to be knowledge appropriate for teaching children. The demonstration indicated to them what they might look for, and the students engaged in a range of practical activities.

Each of the seven teaching groups was given textual information, diagrams, and globes of the earth and models of earth's rotation. They used the models to match up to various diagrams. A science tutor then explained what was happening to the earth, sun or moon at a particular point. Some students, using the torches and globes, were quickly able to understand what was happening and explain it. The explanation and answering questions helped them to reconstruct their understanding. Others repeated again and again what they were doing to try and make sense of the knowledge presented to them.

These findings are consistent with those of Stella Vosniadou (1997) who has looked at children from India, Greece, Samoa and the USA to consider their perceptions about earth. They illustrate a number of important points about developing science concepts such as the earth and space. Although much of 'Earth in Space' is not covered within the National Curriculum, teachers need to understand these wider concepts in order to explain the parts that are there. For example, length of shadows requires an understanding of how the sun's position in the sky varies.

The students also appreciated that science learning is a process of continually developing concept understanding. For many of these students returning to a science topic covered in secondary school and finding that they needed to reinvestigate what they thought they knew came as a surprise. As students' understanding of these planetary interrelationships developed they could see the need for a variety of teaching methods. From their own experiences as learners the students saw they needed many resources and ways of working with them to allow all learners to engage in the concept and restructure their existing knowledge. OFSTED (1997) refers to teachers' lack of knowledge, bringing home how problematic science knowledge is. The following selections from OFSTED indicate the weaknesses they found in primary science as well as what represented good learning.

OFSTED Inspection findings (1997)

- I in 8 primary teachers have insufficient expertise in science
- I in 7 schools have a weakness in science resources
- I school in 6 is weak in science, particularly at upper KS2
- I school in 6 science lessons lack pace and challenge particularly at Y2 and Y6
- I school in 4 has a weakness in science planning
- I school in 4 science assessment is weak at KSI especially Y2
- I school in 3 science assessment is weak at KS2 especially Y5/6
- POSI and 0 are less well developed than knowledge
- Pupils' abilities to predict outcomes, seek patterns, evaluate results are poor.

Pupils do many excellent science activities but do not sufficiently develop their investigative skills. (My italics)

OFSTED (1997) Quality of Learning

Where learning is good, most pupils respond to the challenge of the tasks set, show a willingness to concentrate on them and make good progress. They adjust well to the demands of working in different contexts, selecting appropriate methods and organising effectively the resources they need. Work is sustained with a sense of commitment and enjoyment. Pupils are sufficiently confident and alert to raise questions and to persevere with their work when answers are not readily available. They evaluate their own work and come to realistic judgments about it. Where appropriate, pupils readily help one another.

Learning science

The example discussed above seems to be consistent across several cultures and indicates the complexity of learning science. There seems to be agreement amongst researchers that:

■ Learning science is difficult. Students experience difficulty with concepts, even at undergraduate level. It is important that children get a good introduction to science during their primary schooling.

■ Learning science is plagued with misconceptions. The teacher must judge when to ask questions, which promote further investigation, and when to support with factual scientific information, thus 'scaffolding' the learner so that their misconception is challenged, the science understood and the existing knowledge restructured.

■ Learning science uses inert knowledge. This is knowledge that is known but may not be used when it is relevant. This is a particular issue in primary schools where the culture can be centred on linguistic and creative development. When a child is involved in practical science and writing about their work, the teacher needs to be aware of and make explicit that those scientific processes, concepts, methods and vocabulary are explicitly used and described. It is common for children to write about what they did 'we got out all the magnets and played with them' rather than write about the effects that were observed – the actual science. Teachers may need to be explicit in their planning to ensure they are aware of and address this issue.

■ Learning science involves the development of science concepts, the science knowledge and the development of process skills and investigational abilities. Some lessons may be explicitly for process skill development, others to gain knowledge to understand a particular concept.

Enquiry task 3

What science do you know?

As a teacher you need to be aware of how you take your knowledge for granted but that pupils will not share that knowledge.

Choose an area of science you are familiar with. Take an A3 sheet of paper, on the left side rule a margin about 5cm wide. Now choose a specific aspect of science with which you are familiar, for example photosynthesis, food chains, electricity, DNA, atomic structure, try not to make it too broad.
1 In the column on the left write down all the words that come to mind about that science concept.
2 Using the rest of the A3 sheet write the words from your list and use arrows to link words. Along the arrow write in any scientific links of which you are aware. The concept map should indicate the science you know within that particular topic.

---

3 Now look closely at your map, are there gaps, areas of few connections? Are there lots of arrows showing links but little to explain those links. Do you need to research this subject some more? Using resource books can you research and add extra areas to your map? Use a different colour for these new words, statements and arrows.
4 Are there any words or phrases you would find difficult to explain to a child? If there are, how will you overcome this?

Teachers of primary science need a wide ranging understanding of scientific concepts and the process skills that support concept development. They need to be aware of the complexity for pupils of learning science and a wide range of teaching strategies to support that learning. Additionally, they have to make value judgments as to how their teaching enables learning and supports the curriculum. Learning to think and work scientifically supports cognitive development. It is a powerful tool in understanding the world. Science encourages a questioning, logical and systematic approach. Practical, investigative activities develop a wide range of communicative skills through children co-operating with others, sharing ideas and reporting on their findings. Science is a process of continuous learning both for teacher and child. Every time a child asks a science question the teacher's own understanding of the scientific concept or process skill application develops. Each successful explanation is another tool in the teacher's kit.

References

ASSOCIATION FOR SCIENCE EDUCATION (1993) *Primary Science Teachers Handbook*, SHERRINGTON, R. (ed.), London: ASE.

ATKINSON, S. and FLEER, M. (1995) *Science with Reason*, London: Hodder and Stoughton.

CARRE, C. and OVENS, C. (1994) *Science 7 to 11: Developing Primary Teaching Skills*, London: Routledge.

DFE (1995) *Key Stages 1 and 2 of the National Curriculum*, London. HMSO.

FEASEY, R. in SHERRINGTON, R. (1993) *ASE Primary Science Teachers Handbook*, London: Simon and Schuster.

FENSHAM P., GUNSTONE, R. and WHITE, R. (eds) (1995) *The Content of Science*, London: Falmer Press.

FILKIN, D. (1997) *Stephen Hawking's Universe: The Cosmos Explained*, London: BBC Books.

HARLEN, W. (1996) *The Teaching of Science in Primary Schools*, London: David Fulton.

HARLEN, W. (1997) 'Criteria for identifying progression in scientific ideas for primary school pupils' in HARNQVIST, K. and BURGEN, A. (eds) *Growing Up with Science*, Bristol: Jessica Kingsley Publishers.

HARNQVIST, K. and Burgen, A. (eds) (1997) *Growing up with Science*, Bristol: Jessica Kingsley Publishers.

HOLLINS, M. and WHITBY, V. (1998) *Progression in Primary Science. A Guide to the Nature and Practice of Science in Key Stages 1 and 2*, London: David Fulton.

McCUNE, R. (1998) 'Science education for the year 2000 and beyond', *Education in Science*, **176**, February 1998, Hatfield: ASE.

NUFFIELD PRIMARY SCIENCE (1997) *Science Co-ordinators' Manual*, London: Nuffield.

OFSTED (1997) *Inspection Reports for Key Stage 1 and Key Stage 2*, London: HMSO.

OFSTED (1998) *Standards in Primary Science*, London: OFSTED Publications.

PEACOCK, A. (1997) *Opportunities for Science in the Primary School*, Staffordshire: Trentham Books.

QCA (1984–91) *The Children's Learning in Science Project* (CLISP), London: QCA.

RITCHIE, R. and OLLERENSHAW, C. (1997) *Primary Science: Making It Work*, London: David Fulton.

SMITH, R. and PEACOCK, G. (1995) *Investigations and Progression in Science*, London: Hodder & Stoughton.

SMITH, R. and PEACOCK, G. (1992) *Teaching and Understanding Science*, London: Hodder and Stoughton.

TUOMI, J. (1997) *National Science Education Standards. Science Education Reform in the United States*, in HARNQVIST, K. and BURGEN, A. (eds) *Growing Up with Science*, Bristol: Jessica Kingsley Publishers.

UNIVERSITY OF LIVERPOOL (1990–1998) *Primary Science Processes and Concept Exploration (SPACE) Project*, Liverpool: Liverpool University Press.

UNIVERSITY OF OXFORD, WESTMINSTER COLLEGE (1993) Understanding Science Concepts, Primary Teachers and Science (PSTS) Project, Oxford: OUP.

VOSNIADOU, S. (1997) 'On the development of the understanding of abstract ideas', in HARNQVIST, K. and BURGEN, A. (Eds) *Growing Up with Science*, Bristol: Jessica Kingsley Publishers.

Notes on contributors

Kate Ashcroft is Professor and Dean of Education in the University of the West of England. She is joint series editor of 'Looking Afresh at the Primary Curriculum' of which this book is a part. She is co-author of '*Implementing the Primary Curriculum: A Teacher's Guide*' and '*The Primary Teacher's Guide to the New Curriculum*'. She has also researched and published on teaching, learning and quality in higher education.

Helen Butcher taught for 15 years as a Key Stage 1 specialist and English subject leader in inner city and rural primary schools. She is currently Senior Lecturer in Education at the University of the West of England and coordinates professional English and Advanced Early Years Courses. She is currently researching the development of early literacies in young children.

Bernadette Fitzgerald is Senior Lecturer in Education in the University of the West of England and is responsible for the secondary PGCE English course. She also teaches professional English to primary students. She worked with the LINC project and is co-author of '*Looking into Language*' and '*The Language of Reading*'. Currently she is working on the development of the National Literacy Strategy for Key Stage 3 pupils.

Gordon Guest is Senior Lecturer in primary science and primary design and technology in the University of the West of England. He is involved in both initial teacher training and inservice education. Formerly he was a primary classroom teacher, Deputy Headteacher and Headteacher and was also Science Curriculum Development Officer for Service Children's Schools in Germany. He has also taught in Botswana. His current research interest is in the field of teaching and learning in primary science.

John Lee is Principal Lecturer in Education in the University of the West of England. He teaches English and classroom management on primary courses. He has recently co-edited '*Managing Special Needs in Mainstream Schools*' and is currently researching the impact of the literacy hour classroom on pupils with special needs. He has researched and published extensively on school inspection and national policy.

Keith Postlethwaite is Professor of Education in the University of the West of England. He has researched and published extensively in the fields of special educational needs and provision for the most able. He is also an active researcher in science education and teaching professional learning.

Ruth Sharpe is Senior Lecturer in Education in the University of the West of England where she is responsible for coordinating the teaching of primary mathematics. She is presently researching teaching and learning mathematics in early years classrooms. Currently she is conducting work on the teaching of numeracy in primary classrooms on behalf of the Teacher Training Agency.

Index

diction 53
digraphs 45
direct teaching 106–7
discovery orientation 94
distance learning materials 36
double negatives 11
drafting 63, 65–6
drama lessons 30
Driver, R. 128, 135, 143

Education Act (1944) 128
Education Reform Act (ERA 1988) 16, 17, 25, 91
effectiveness 33, 36
electricity 151–2, 158–9
engineering 12
English 6, 8, 11, 14
 core subjects 24
 disputes 25
 monitoring 19–20
 National Curriculum 30, 31
 NC introduction 18
 programmes of study 53
 standards 19, 21–2
 surveys 16–17
enquiry tasks
 core subjects 7, 8, 10
 curriculum comparison 17, 18–19
 genres 73, 85
 grammar 43, 54
 guided reading 40
 literacy hour 7, 36
 mathematics 93, 95, 99
 numeracy 114, 118, 120–1
 pedagogy 35
 planning 46
 SATs results 22, 23
 science 130, 145, 155, 160, 168–9
 spoken language 57, 60–2
 teaching time 20
 word level 44–5
 written language 60, 61, 62
entitlement 16, 48
environment 149, 151
equality 3

Ernest, P. 90, 91
essay-writing 79
everyone reading in class (ERIC) 41
Exel project 43
exploratory learning 16
expressive arts 7

Faraday, M. 126
Farrell, S. 92
Fermat's last theorem 9
field 77
Finland 26
Fitzgerald, B. 53–66
flash cards 44
floating 13, 143
formative assessment 61–2, 162
foundation subjects 16, 17, 129
France 48
free school meals 48
Freyberg, P. 126, 135

Gagné, R. 141–2
gases 165
genres 4, 33, 39, 42–3, 56, 69–86
geography 16, 17
GEST 101
girls 22
glossary of terms 56–7
goals 49, 70
good practice 31, 39, 49, 128
Goodman, K. 28
Goswami, U. 45
governors 36
grammar 11–12, 14, 25, 34, 53–66
 shared reading 38–9
 teaching methods 43
graphic knowledge 38
Graves, D. 28
Great Debate 121
Greece 167
Griffiths, H. B. 88, 90
Guesne, E. 128
Guest, G. 126–46, 149–69
guided reading 38–41, 48
guided writing 43